1 MONTH OF
FREE
READING

at

www.ForgottenBooks.com

By purchasing this book you are eligible for one month membership to ForgottenBooks.com, giving you unlimited access to our entire collection of over 1,000,000 titles via our web site and mobile apps.

To claim your free month visit:

www.forgottenbooks.com/free961140

ISBN 978-0-260-63715-4
PIBN 10961140

JOINT DOCUMENTS

OF THE

STATE OF MICHIGAN,

FOR THE YEAR 1853.

BY AUTHORITY.

LANSING:

GEO. W. PECK, PRINTER TO THE STATE.

1854.

CONTENTS.

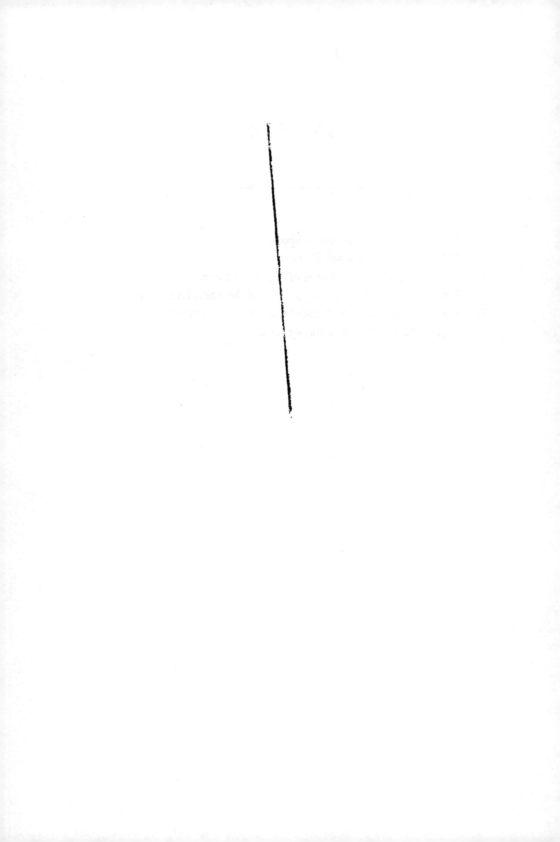

STATE OF MICHIGAN.

1853.

DOCUMENT No. 1.

AUDITOR GENERAL'S ANNUAL REPORT.

Auditor General's Office, }
Lansing, Mich., Dec. 1, 1853. }

To His Excellency, Andrew Parsons, *acting Governor of the State of Michigan:*

Sir—In obedience to the requirements of Act No. 161, Laws of 1851, I have the honor to submit the following

REPORT:

It will be seen by the following statement of the receipts and expenditures for the last fiscal year, that there is now on hand in the State Treasury, $375,773 68. This large surplus will, no doubt, be soon increased, by receipts into the Treasury from various sources, to over a half million of dollars.

Notwithstanding this encouraging exhibit of the State finances, the present safe keeping, and ultimate proper application of so large a surplus, must be a source of anxious solicitude. With such unparalleled progress in individual wealth and prosperity, an overflowing Treasury, and a forgetfulness of the financial embarrassments from which the State has just been extricated, it is to be feared, may lead us into imprudent appropriations, if not into extravagant and wasteful expenditures of the public money. In credit abroad and in prosperity at home,

1

in climate and in soil, in her mineral resources and commercial advantages, and above all, in her Educational interests, Michigan occupies a high position among her sisters of the Union. Let not imprudence, extravagance or cupidity, again reduce her to financial embarrassment.

RECEIPTS AND EXPENDITURES FOR THE YEAR ENDING NOVEMBER 30, 1853.

The balance in the hands of the State Treasurer on Nov. 30, 1852, exclusive of amounts to meet outstanding warrants upon the General and Primary School Interest Funds, was......................$116,407 23

	Expended.	Received.
General Fund,	$205,833 12	$373,515 51
Internal Improvement Fund,	112,404 92	74,952 14
University Fund,		34,984 44
University Interest Fund,	15,105 45	11,287 97
State Building Fund,		2,651 21
Primary School Fund,		107,417 20
Primary School Interest Fund,	54,517 06	43,664 65
Contingent Fund,	214 00	
Asylum Fund,	1,993 49	1,710 91
Normal School Fund,	1,479 57	3,909 79
Normal School Interest Fund,	3,731 38	1,319 04
Sault Ste. Marie Canal Fund,	1,071 92	
Swamp Land Fund,	2 80	
Central Railroad Deposits,	80 68	
Southern Railroad Deposits,	15 00	
St. Joseph Valley Railroad Deposits,		255 00
* Balance charged State Treasurer, Nov. 30, 1853,	375,625 70	
	$772,075 09	$772,075 09

EXHIBIT OF FUNDS.

The foregoing table shows the several funds belonging to the State, all of which will be treated of under their appropriate heads.

---

* Add to this amount $147 98, for outstanding warrants, which will make $375,773 68, the amount in the hands of the State Treasurer, Nov. 30, 1853.

GENERAL FUND.

EXPENDITURES.

Salaries Public officers,	$12,959 07
Stationery Public offices,	5,589 86
Furniture "	122 94
Postage	920 97
State Library,	49 50
Incidental expenses Public offices,	1,207 75
General appropriation Leg. of 1850,	1 50
Sundry awards of Board State Auditors,	1,112 19
General appropriation Leg. of 1851,	95 00
Holders General Fund Bonds,	27,060 00
" University Bonds,	5,640 00
" Penitentiary Bonds,	3,600 00
Fugitives from justice,	238 72
Coroners' fees,	301 45
Wolf bounty,	954 00
District canvass,	188 40
Repairs and supplies Leg. Halls,	1,407 28
Leg. printing and pub'g laws,	7,565 99
Printing paper,	1,376 00
Volunteer regiment,	367 84
Expense Leg. 1853,	21,148 23
" 1850,	22 82
Surplus refunded,	35 95
Exchange	2 75
Gen'l appropriation Leg. 1848,	1 50
Delinquent taxes refunded,	2,039 55
" " interest refunded,	539 80
Office charges refunded,	19 93
State bids refunded,	1,686 92
" interest refunded,	336 51
State tax lands refunded,	2,682 08
" interest refunded,	85 97
Redemption money refunded,	15,962 49
Fire proof offices,	9,054 13
Apppropriation act 133, 1851,	155 06

Appropriation act 134, 1851,	$230	00
Costs of suits,	33	11
Improvements at Lansing,	889	12
Mining Company tax, paid to Houghton County,	3,499	00
Paid sundry Counties,	26,585	00
Expenses State prison,	9,500	00
Expense of sales, refunded and disbursed from proceeds of sales,	23,674	10
New Capitol buildings, (repairs,)	1,409	99
Expense Electoral College,	228	00
" Supreme Court,	15,254	20
Total,	$205,833	12

RECEIPTS.

For old furniture,	$4	00
For Books lost from State Library,	30	87
Proceeds of Sales,	107,739	03
Sales Reports of Supreme Court,	50	40
Sales of statutes, &c.,	17	25
Delinquent taxes,	38,612	50
Delinquent taxes, interest,	3,109	27
Office charges,	2,590	94
State bids,	6,905	68
State bids, interest,	1,176	97
State tax lands,	3,942	44
State tax lands, interest,	267	45
Redemptions, (individual,)	9,444	62
Redemptions, (State,)	4,966	20
Expense of sales,	1,553	93
Brokers' license,	415	50
Pedlars' license,	193	02
Salt Spring lands,	1,363	35
Telegraph specific tax,	63	75
Bank specific tax,	9,385	96
Of United States on account of volunteer regiment,	21,731	06
Rail Road specific tax,	79,408	06
Plank Road specific tax,	1,239	95
Mining Companies' specific tax,	11,841	43

From sundry counties,............................... 67,461 38
For drawing paper,.................................   50

Total,.......................................$373,515 51

Since the date of my last Annual Report, a settlement of our claim against the United States for moneys advanced for the Michigan Regiment of Volunteers, in the Mexican war, has been effected, and the amount ($21,731 06) has been received by the State Treasurer.

The interest on the General Fund, University, and Penitentiary Bonds, will be promptly paid when due, on presentation of the coupons at the Phœnix Bank in New York City.

The appropriation from this Fund, made by the last Legislature for Fire Proof Offices, has been expended, and the building is nearly ready for use.

INTERNAL IMPROVEMENT FUND.

	Dr.	Cr.
To balance, Dec. 1, 1852,.............	$430,940 90	
" interest on five million loan bonds,...	8,970 00	
" " Int. Imp. warrant bonds,...	2,011 33	
" " Det. &. Pont. R. R. bonds,.	8,750 00	
" " adjusted bonds,...........	19,778 19	
" " Treasury notes,...........	35	
" " Int. Imp. warrants,.......	683 56	
" bonds paid in,...................	70,239 75	
" Rec'd for asset land, refunded,......	150 00	
" land warrants issued,.............	6,671 87	
" exchange,......................	564 10	
" paid award to S. W. Pitts,..........	50 00	
By rec'd of United States for 5 per cents., on sales of public lands,...........		$10,328 17
" Int. Imp. lands sold,.............		4,153 97
" Asset lands sold,................		720 00
" Instalments and int. rec'd from Mich. Sou. R. R. Co.,.................		59,750 00
" appropriation act No. 160, 1851,....		75,000 00
" debit balance, Dec. 1, 1853,.......		393,857 91
Total,........................	$543,810 05	$543,810 05

The $7,260 of Interest Bonds, mentioned in my last Report, due January 1, 1850, have been surrendered and paid. Provision has also been made at the Phœnix Bank, for the prompt payment of the interest as it becomes due on the Five Million Loan, Detroit and Pontiac Railroad, and Adjusted Bonds. The interest on all the outstanding Internal Improvement Warrant Bonds has been stopped. The whole amount of interest on this class of Bonds, unpaid, is $769 28. This interest will be paid on presentation of the coupons to the State Treasury, if the full amount of semi-annual interest is due, or upon a surrender of the Bonds, if only a portion is due.

TRUST FUNDS.

	Receipts.	Expenditures.
Primary school fund,..................	$107,417 20	
" interest fund,............	43,664 65	$54,517 06
University fund,.....................	34,984 44	
" interest fund,..............	11,287 97	15,105 45
Normal school fund,..................	3,909 79	1,479 57
" interest fund,...........	1,319 04	3,731 38
Swamp land fund,....................		2 80
Saut Ste. Marie Canal fund,...........		1,071 92
Michigan Central Railroad deposits,.....		80 68
" Southern "		15 00
St. Joseph Valley "	255 00	
Asylum fund,........................	1,710 91	1,993 49
Total,........................	$204,549 00	$77,997 35

The amount now due by the State to the Primary School Fund is $378,028 77—showing an increase of this class of indebtedness during the past year, of over $100,000. The receipts into the Treasury on account of other educational funds, present a corresponding degree of prosperity.

The total amount due from the State to the University Fund is $73,504 46. In addition to the interest on this sum, the last Legislature (Act No. 60) required the Auditor General to draw his warrant on the State Treasurer for interest on $100,000 of bonds, heretofore issued by the State, for the benefit of the University, and upon which the State pays interest to the holders thereof—thus making the

State pay double interest on that amount. This is the plain and simple meaning of the act, although it is so drawn up, as in a measure to disguise the fact. It is true the act is limited to the period of two years, and if it was only intended by those officers of the University who drafted the bill, as a donation to the University of $14,000, to relieve it from present embarrassment, it is well—but if it was intended as a precedent for future legislative action, it is wrong. It would bring the State in debt to the University $100,000, in addition to the $73,504 46 above stated to be due, and the State would also have to pay the $100,000 bonds heretofore assumed. If this claim be a good one, then a claim for the entire amount of interest from the issuing of those bonds in 1839 to the present and for all future time, would be good. Are the people of this State prepared to sanction and allow such a claim? Are they prepared to take so large an amount from the State Treasury for an institution whose annual income is now over $25,000, and rapidly increasing?—a sum in all conscience, amply sufficient for an economical administration of its affairs.

CONTINGENT FUND.

The balance in the Treasury Nov. 30, 1852, was $9,872 61. By Joint Resolution No. 15, of the last session, all but $1000 was transferred to the General Fund. There is now a balance of $786 00 yet unexpended.

SWAMP LAND FUND.

The expenditures on account of the Swamp Land Fund are $655 30, for maps, books, and clerk hire, preparatory to the sales on the 13th December. It is believed that at the sales, at least $50,000 will be received to the credit of this Fund.

The amount received into the Treasury, by Act No. 187, Laws of 1851, is loaned to the State. The State is to pay interest on the amount so received, and this interest also becomes a part of the fund aforesaid. When the swamp lands in the northern districts of the State are brought into market, the fund will be largely increased. The final and proper disposition of this fund, so that all may participate in its benefits, is a matter of great importance to the State. It is a question which should be taken into serious consideration by the people in the selection of their Representatives to the next Legislature; for by imprudent legislation, this princely fund may be worse than squandered.

It was evidently the design of the legislative committee, who had the bill in charge in 1851, to ultimately appropriate the nett proceeds from the sale of these lands to educational purposes. Such a disposition will be eminently just and proper—the whole people will reap a rich reward in the annual distribution of the interest of the fund, for the education of the rising generation. And now, that this immense fund is within our grasp, it is to be hoped that future legislators will act with equal patriotism, and frown upon any attempt by interested parties to appropriate it for less important purposes.

SAULT STE. MARIE CANAL FUND.

Section 5 of the act to provide for the construction of a Ship Canal around the Falls of St. Mary, provides that the contractor or contractors for the construction of said canal shall defray the entire cost of surveying, locating, and constructing the same, the necessary travelling and other expenses of the commissioners, and the salary of the engineer and assistants. The same section provides for the payment of these expenses out of the State Treasury, and that the same shall be reimbursed by the contractors, as fast as ascertained, under the direction of the Commissioners. The State has advanced $1,071 92; other accounts have been presented, but I have refused to allow them, until the above amount shall be reimbursed.

A clause exempting the lands granted by Congress from taxation while in the hands of contractors, was struck out of the original bill before it became a law; but a few days after, a supplemental bill was passed, not merely *exempting* the lands from taxation, but *remitting* the taxes after assessment and return, and directing the Auditor General to give a receipt therefor, and charge the same to the General Fund: "*Provided,* That the amount so charged to the General Fund may be reimbursed to the State from tolls upon said canal, in such manner as shall be provided by law, in case said amount shall not be reimbursed by the United States Government."

By this proviso, before the Auditor General can give a receipt, as above contemplated, it must be first ascertained whether the United States will reimburse this amount, and also whether the Legislature shall provide for a reimbursement from tolls upon said canal. In the meantime the lands may be returned for non-payment of taxes, sold, and past redemption; thus placing it beyond the power of the Auditor

General to give a receipt. Had the provisions of this supplemental bill been well considered, I think it could not have met with the approval of the Legislature and the late Governor. The contractors, to enhance the value of their lands, may procure the taxation of them to any amount, for the construction of roads, and the building of bridges and school-houses, and the United States or this State must pay for it, or it must become a heavy tax upon the carrying trade of the Upper Peninsula, in the shape of tolls on the canal. There can be no doubt that the magnificent donation of 750,000 acres of land would have been amply sufficient to have secured the early completion of the canal, without any such supplemental bill.

STATE INDEBTEDNESS.

The funded and fundable debt not yet due, is as follows:

General Fund bonds, due May, 1856,	$100,000 00
University bonds, due July, 1858,	99,000 00
Detroit & Pontiac Rail Road bonds, due July, 1858,	97,000 00
Penitentiary bonds, due January, 1859,	20,000 00
Penitentiary bonds, due January, 1860,	40,000 00
Full paid $5,000,000 loan bonds, due January, 1863,	177,000 00
Adjusted bonds, due January, 1863,	342,391 00
Total,	$875,391 00

The part paid $5,000,000 loan bonds outstanding, will, if funded previous to January 1, 1854, amount to, ..$1,457,001 07
Bonds issuable for outstanding I. I. warrants, say, ... 7,000 00

Making the total funded and fundable debt not yet due, and for the payment of which no provision is made, ..$2,339,392 07
The amount due the trust funds, is 466,956 26

All the Internal Improvement Warrant bonds heretofore issued, have been advertised for, and interest stopped. All but $32,850 of these bonds have been surrendered and paid. A large proportion of those yet outstanding, are held by the banks as security for their circulating notes, although their charters require a deposit of interest-paying bonds.

Only $28,000 of part paid bonds have been surrendered during the past fiscal year. Adjusted bonds were issued therefor to the amount of $15,377 32. Of this amount $13,729 75, being redeemable at the

2

option of the State under a law passed by the last Legislature, were surrendered and paid. All the adjusted bonds hereafter issued for part paid bonds surrendered will be made redeemable at the option of the State. Whatever amount may be funded, the surplus in the treasury will be immediately used for its liquidation.

The hope so long entertained, that the offer made by the State to the holders of this class of bonds by Act No. 173, Laws of 1848, would induce them to surrender their bonds for adjustment, has not been realized. The Constitution prohibits the funding of these bonds beyond the amount fixed by the aforesaid act, and the holders can no longer reasonably entertain any hope of increasing it. Interest, however, is continually accruing on the amount due on these bonds at the rate of 7 per cent. per annum until funded, when it forms a part of the principal of the adjusted bonds issuable therefor. This may be a sufficient inducement for capitalists to withhold them from adjustment. I therefore suggest the propriety of requesting the Legislature to so modify the proposition in the law of 1848, as to stop interest on all part paid bonds not surrendered for adjustment within a given time. This will prevent the increase of our unfunded debt, and it can be no hardship to the holder, for by an immediate surrender, he will receive adjusted bonds for the amount originally received by the State with interest to the January succeeding the funding, and he will thereafter receive interest semi-annually, unless sooner redeemed.

All the State indebtedness, (except what are termed Part Paid Bonds,) a redemption of which can be compelled, or interest stopped, was called in last year; and as our Bonds are above par, none can be purchased under our present laws. There is, therefore, no further opportunity of liquidating State indebtedness with the surplus on hand, except by paying up what few Part Paid Bonds may be voluntarily surrendered. The prospect of so large a surplus lying idle in the Treasury, was a source of much anxiety during the last session of the Legislature. In view of the exigencies of the case, that body passed, and the late Governor, Hon. R. McClelland, approved, on the 9th day of February last, an act requiring the depositaries of these funds to pay interest thereon at a rate of not less than five per cent. per annum; but the same Legislature, *at the solicitation of the depositaries,* or by "*some strange and unaccountable overturn of justice,*" on the 12th day of February, only three days after the passage of the above act, passed a supplementary act, which was also approved by the late Governor, reducing the rate to one per cent. per annum. The result is, the banks in which the surplus is deposited, pay interest to the State at the rate of one per cent. per annum, while the State has to pay at the rate of six per cent. on her funded debt, and seven per cent. on her unfunded debt. This is all wrong—the Legislature should have provided for some disposition of the surplus funds, whereby the State should realize the same amount of interest that she pays, until those funds could be used in liquidation of State indebtedness.

STATE BOARD OF EQUALIZATION.

This Board met at the Capital, on the 15th day of August, last, as required by Act No. 97, Laws of 1858. A meeting of the State Board at that time was rendered necessary by the re-enactment, with highly important and beneficial amendments, of our entire system of taxation. For the result of their labors see statement No. 9 of the appendix.

The beneficial working of the system, has exceeded the most sanguine anticipations of its warmest friends, notwithstanding the most violent opposition, for a short time, was arrayed against it, i y interested parties. In consequence of this opposition, and in view of the fact that the law which had not yet had time to be disseminated among the people, was being misrepresented and misinterpreted, I issued several circulars, (see latter part of appendix,) that there might be greater uniformity in the action of the assessing officers. The result has been highly satisfactory. A large majority of the Supervisors have faithfully discharged their duties, under the law. If, under this first assessment, any inequalities shall be discovered, the cause can be traced directly to a non-compliance with the law on the part of the tax-payer, or the assessing officer. A full, faithful and impartial compliance with the law must result in equality—and equality is the great object to be attained by any system of taxation.

A large number of delegates from the several counties were in attendance before the Board, and after close observation and careful investigation, they were of the opinion that only a few slight amendments were necessary, to perfect the law; in this opinion the Board unanimously concurred.

The aggregate value of real and personal estate for 1851, was $30
976,270 18; for 1853, the first assessment under the new law, it
$120,362,474 35. It is believed that with the experience of the pa
year, and a better understanding of the law, the next assessment w
be still more satisfactory.

The clause requiring sales for delinquent taxes one year sooner th
heretofore, has had a beneficial effect, especially upon the new countie
It has enabled them to redeem their outstanding county orders, and t
pay the townships the amounts their due for delinquent highway an
school taxes, one year sooner than it could otherwise have been don
The non-resident tax-payer can have no good cause for complaint, f
he yet has one year and eight months longer time in which to pay h
taxes, than the resident.

The clause prohibiting the offering of twice-offered State tax land
for what they would bring, has saved thousands of dollars to the Stat
The loss from the sale of this class of State tax lands, in Oct. 185
was about $25,000. This loss had to be made up by direct tax up
the people. Under the present law, these lands must be sold for th
entire amount of tax, interest and expenses, or remain the property o
the State. It is probable that the State will soon dispose of her Stat
tax lands, as, since the decision of the Supreme Court, throwing th
burthen of proof upon the claimant against a tax title, more confidenc
in the title to these lands is manifest, and they are greedily sought fo

If our tax laws are insufficient to convey a good title, then non-res
-dents will refuse to pay their taxes, and the whole burthen of taxatio
will be thrown upon the residents of the State. If all the tax titles ar
void, justice requires the State to refund to the purchasers their purcha
money and interest. To do this, would require a greater sum tha
the entire amount of our State indebtedness. There may be isolated
cases of hardship under the decision of the Supreme Court above r
ferred to, but he who refuses or neglects to contribute his just proportion for the support of the government which protects his property, i
deserving of no sympathy.

SPECIFIC TAXES.

The entire amount of specific taxes except that received from the
mining companies, during the past fiscal year, is $90,706 24. Thes
taxes by article 14 of the Constitution, must be " applied in paying

e interest upon the Primary School, University and other educational
nds, and the interest on the State debt;" the balance, if any, is to be
pplied in payment of the principal of the State debt. The interest
e past fiscal year amounted to $84,691 60—leaving $6,014 64 to
a applied in liquidation of State indebtedness.

For detail of all specific taxes see statement No. 7.

RAILROAD SPECIFIC TAX.

The amount of specific tax paid in by the railroad companies during
e last fiscal year, is $79,408 06. On the 11th day of February, 1853,
e Southern Railroad Company paid in on account of specific tax for the
current year, $22,578 22. The Company stood charged on the books
f this office with $24,562 11; the Treasurer was written to, and the
alance was immediately forwarded. The Central Railroad Company
ere charged on their last report, for tax of 1853, $62,178 43; only
51,751 84 was paid in. On the 19th day of February, and again on the
4th day of May last, the Treasurer of the Company was notified of
he balance, but receiving no answer, on the 24th day of August last, I
sued a warrant, under a law of last winter, directed to the Sheriff of
Wayne County, for the collection of said balance. I then received a
supplemental report from the Company, showing the amount expended
out of the State, and an offer to pay the balance after deducting the
amount so expended with interest, together with all expenses that
had accrued. This offer was accepted, and the amount (2,677 86)
has been paid into the Treasury.

The Detroit and Pontiac Railroad Company is indebted to the State
on account of specific taxes for 1851, 1852 and 1853. A portion of
he tax for those years, has been paid, and I am informed by the Treasurer that the balance will be soon adjusted.

The tax on the Erie & Kalamazoo Railroad Company is included in
he amount paid in by the Southern Railroad Company.

BANK SPECIFIC TAX.

The amount of Bank tax paid in during the year, is $9,385 96.
The last report from this office stated that "the stocks deposited by
some of the Banks, for which they receive circulating notes, exceeds the
amount of their capital stock reported, and upon this excess it is claimed
they are exempt from taxation. If this be the correct view, then there
is no limit to their circulation, and with a capital of only $100,000, up-

on which they pay tax, they may deposit stocks with the Treasurer, and do a business of millions upon which they would pay no tax. It was no doubt the intention of the Legislature to limit the stock and circulation to $500,000. I have therefore charged a tax, in the cases above referred to, on the amount of stocks deposited; but the Michigan Insurance, Peninsular, and Government Stock Banks, have only paid on the capital stock they report to have paid in, causing a loss to the State, the past year, of over $3,000." Soon after the date of that report, the Government Stock Bank paid in the amount with which it stood charged on the books of this office for 1852. The Peninsular Bank has also paid, but under protest. For 1853, the Banks were charged a specific tax upon the same principle as for 1852; but the Government Stock and Michigan Insurance Banks refused to pay, except upon the capital stock they report to have paid in. Warrants have been issued for the collection of the balance; but injunctions have been granted, and the question is now before the Supreme Court.

For other specific taxes, see statement No. 7.

BROKERS' LICENSE.

Of the large number of brokers in the State doing business, only the following have paid license: D. McIntyre, Follett, Conklin & Co., Bidwell & Miles, W. H. Waldby, W. A. Butler, S. H. Ives & Co., C. T. Gorham, Ransom & Dodge, J. C. Bailey, Crippen & Fisk, Ives & Miles, J. A. Weeks & Co., N. H. Wing & Co., L. C. Kellogg and Howard, Smith & Co. The remainder are daily doing business in open violation of law.

STATE TAX FOR 1853.

The State tax for 1853, apportioned among the several counties was $10,000. By Act No. 80, Laws of 1853, $13,000 for the present and $10,000 for the coming year, were appropriated from the General Fund in aid of the Michigan Asylums, to be reimbursed from the proceeds of the sales of lands belonging to the Asylum Fund. In order that the surplus funds might be used solely for the liquidation of any State indebtedness that might be surrendered, at my suggestion, a clause was inserted in the said act, directing the Auditor General to apportion the said amounts as other State taxes were apportioned. But at the time of making the apportionment for 1853, seeing no prospect of using the rapidly accumulating surplus for the purposes above stated, I thought it better policy to use it in aid of the Asylums, until it can be reimbursed, than to raise that amount from the pockets of the people to lie idle in the Treasury.

ACCOUNTS WITH THE COUNTIES.

The whole amount due from the counties for State tax for the present and previous years, is $62,586 05, as will be seen by reference to statement No. 6. Nearly the whole of this amount will be paid by returns of delinquent taxes in February next. Washtenaw county, however, it will be perceived, will be indebted to the State after receiving credit for the February returns, over $10,000—and no provision, I learn, has been made by the supervisors for its liquidation.

The treasurer of Shiawassee county has not yet made return of last October sales—when he does so, the amount due that county will be paid in full. A settlement was made with all the counties to which the State was indebted, at the time the treasurers made their returns, and the full amount due was paid.

In the preceding report I have endeavored to point out some of the errors of the past, as a warning for the future. In conclusion, permit me again to congratulate the people of Michigan upon the bright prospects before them. With an almost entire exemption from taxation for State expenses—with unlimited natural resources—with a soil scarcely equalled in fertility and productiveness—with an enterprising and industrious population, nothing but inexcusable legislative blunders can retard the onward march of our beautiful Peninsula to increased prosperity and usefulness.

JOHN SWEGLES,
Auditor General.

APPENDIX.

APPENDIX

[No. 1.]

*Table of the salaries of State Officers, showing the appropriation
for 1853, and the amounts paid during the past fiscal year.*

	Appropriation for 1853.	Amount paid during the year.
Governor, { R. McClelland, $931 30		
{ A. Parsons, $150 00	$1,000 00	$1,081 30
Secretary of State, W. Graves,	800 00	777 77
State Treasurer, B. C. Whittemore,	1,000 00	1,000 00
Auditor General, J. Swegles,	1,000 00	1,000 00
Commissioner Land Office, P. Kibbee,	800 00	850 00
Sup't Public instruction, F. W. Shearman,	1,000 00	1,100 00
Adjutant General, }	300 00	300 00
Q. Mast'r General, } J. E. Schwarz,	150 00	150 00
Attorney General, W. Hale,	800 00	800 00
State Librarian, { C. J. Fox, $375 00,		
{ C. P. Bush, $125 00	500 00	500 00
Dist. Attorney, Upper Peninsula, J. D. Irvine,	700 00	875 00
Dep. Auditor Gen. and two principal clerks,	1,900 00	1,900 00
Deputy State Treasurer,	700 00	700 00
Deputy Secretary of State,	700 00	675 00
Dep. Com. Land Office and book keeper,	1,300 00	1,250 00
Total,	$12,650 00	$12,959 07

[No. 2.]

Statement of the Expense of the Judiciary.

Daniel Goodwin, Judge,	$1,000 00
David Johnson, "	1,875 00
Joseph T. Copeland, "	1,500 00
Samuel T. Douglas, "	1,500 00
Chas. W. Whipple, "	1,500 00
Warner Wing, "	1,500 00
Abner Pratt, "	1,500 00
Sanford M. Green, "	1,500 00
George Martin, "	1,500 00
Reporter Supreme Court,	875 00
Reports " " Vol. 4,	443 18
Sheriff's fees, stationery, advertising, &c.,	561 07
Total,	$15,254 20

[No. 3.]

Statement of Sales of State Tax Lands, at the Annual Tax Sales, October 3d, 1853.

COUNTIES.	Amount on lists.	Amount above minimum.	Amount sold.	Redeemed or discharged.	Remaining unsold Dec. 1, 1853.
Allegan, ...	$1,559 79	4 92	$619 18	$492 36	$453 17
Barry,.....	1,219 06	....	79 41	306 07	833 58
Berrien....	2,070 93	15 20	621 76	316 98	1,147 39
Branch	401 42	....	26 44	15 12	359 86
Calhoun...	502 08	....	127 44	....	374 64
Cass......	438 99	55	194 49	....	245 05
Clinton....	1,310 57	17 55	188 18	478 91	661 03
Eaton......	127 59	....	60 42	14 72	52 45
Genesee,...	225 10	4 72	68 85	63 57	97 40
Hillsdale...	209 65	....	73 18	16 83	119 64
Ingham,...	429 59	....	49 27	17 94	362 38
Ionia,.....	1,063 81	....	750 90	157 33	155 58
Jackson,...	124 94	....	....	....	124 94
Kalamazoo,.	374 05	....	253 80	86 10	34 15
Kent,.....	1,006 95	....	348 00	189 50	469 45
Lapeer,....	269 90	....	61 62	76 25	132 03
Lenawee...	427 68	....	407 26	20 42	....
Livingston.	642 08	....	586 82	19 70	35 56
Macomb ...	328 93	....	61 48	78 81	188 64
Monroe....	2,343 72	24 44	724 02	453 69	1,190 45
Montcalm..	490 96	....	141 43	30 17	319 36
Oakland,...	539 85	....	206 75	74 39	258 71
Ottawa....	1,786 49	46 58	960 19	289 57	583 31
Saginaw...	1,781 44	....	.63 25	235 92	1,482 27
Shiawassee,.	2,382 32	07	622 74	7 28	1,752 37
St. Clair,...	118 94	....	11 92	35 04	71 98
St. Joseph..	247 24	....	105 67	35 74	105 83
Sanilac,....	312 24	67 96	176 79	30 71	172 70
Tuscola....	226 98	4 41	143 29	37 85	50 25
Van Buren.	41 63	....	....	....	41 63
Washtenaw,	161 73	....	....	....	161 73
Wayne....	2,368 74	....	401 53	111 93	1,155 28
Total,....	$25,535 39	$186 40	$8136 08	$3692 90	$13892 81

[No. 4.]

Statement of Tax Sales Oct. 3d, 1853, for the Taxes of 1851, and unsold descriptions of previous years.

COUNTIES.	Amount advertised.	Paid County Treasurers before sales.	Amount sold.	Bids to State.	Paid or disch'd at Aud. General's Office.
Allegan........	$3,223 22	$395 89	$1,967 61	$769 04	$90 68
Barry	2,606 61	358 78	1,252 94	849 38	145 51
Berrien,......	3,156 29	567 30	1,956 78	588 01	44 20
Branch,.....	1,975 40	405 14	1,167 63	332 91	60 72
Calhoun,.....	2,590 10	338 79	2,102 98	71 05	77 28
Cass, ...	949 32	257 92	415 04	189 79	86 57
Clinton, ...	2,718 33	339 06	1,794 39	415 00	169 88
Eaton	2,348 69	357 48	1,843 95	33 26	114 00
Genesee	2,289 94	335 54	1,783 48	32 91	138 01
Hillsdale,....	2,938 52	569 27	2,181 05	46 04	142 16
Ingham,......	3,435 89	390 48	2,480 62	201 10	343 69
Ionia,........	2,328 52	293 52	1,233 68	567 46	233 86
Jackson,.....	2,649 23	454 83	2,131 13	28 66	34 61
Kalamazoo,...	1,787 48	382 55	842 34	531 49	31 10
Kent	3,854 10	701 37	2,397 14	620 90	134 60
Lapeer	796 88	103 74	562 36	89 75	48 03
Lenawee,....	2,776 85	452 43	2,089 47	....	234 95
Livingston, ...	2,050 03	172 20	1,517 28	46 65	313 90
Macomb, ...	1,292 99	132 01	795 58	227 71	137 60
Monroe,....	4,189 81	864 53	1,064 81	1,071 31	269 16
Montcalm,....	700 70	58 25	154 04	282 04	206 37
Oakland,.....	1,579 59	250 85	1,176 57	86 80	65 37
Ottawa.......	3,650 11	677 87	1,694 95	1,124 31	182 98
Saginaw,.....	3,263 41	456 50	1,067 93	1,339 76	399 22
Shiawassee,...	4,438 16	489 81	2,515 05	1,160 23	273 07
St. Clair,.....	2,842 69	353 38	2,105 22	52 40	331 59
St. Joseph,....	1,196 49	169 90	877 88	93 12	55 59
Sanilac	1,275 50	61 95	640 49	232 24	340 82
Tuscola,.....	646 97	220 27	138 55	263 04	25 11
Van Buren,...	1,993 61	394 06	1,447 02	82 39	140 14
Washtenaw,...	1,165 36	136 95	976 71	20 67	31 03
Wayne	2,317 67	382 83	1,303 76	573 47	57 62
Total,......	$75,028 46	$11,455 45	$46,578 53	$12,015 89	$4,978 58

[No. 5.]

Statement of Tax Sales, Oct. 3d, 1853, for the taxes of 1852.

COUNTIES.	Amount advertised.	Paid Co. Treasurer before sales.	Amount sold.	Bids to State.	Paid or disch'd at Auditor Gen.'s Office.
Allegan,.....	$5,179 22	$697 79	$2,275 62	$1,790 83	$414 96
Barry,.......	3,978 82	677 15	1,531 29	1,508 22	202 06
Berrien,.....	3,984 15	1,177 03	1,730 61	1,015 07	61 44
Branch,.....	2,935 85	739 56	1,423 04	608 82	214 42
Calhoun,.....	3,558 02	639 24	2,432 43	59 74	426 61
Cass,.......	1,219 49	294 25	474 48	350 24	170 52
Clinton,.....	4,604 09	579 56	2,210 82	1,363 94	449 77
Eaton,.......	3,311 70	439 12	2,532 95	23 59	316 02
Genesee,.....	4,777 68	1,163 31	3,151 05	36 61	426 11
Hillsdale,....	3,919 49	855 33	2,881 26	25 70	157 20
Ingham,.....	4,333 75	567 14	3,073 31	116 33	576 97
Ionia,........	3,622 30	592 78	1,494 27	1,180 39	424 96
Jackson,.....	2,397 71	396 10	1,841 79	48 45	111 37
Kalamazoo,...	2,403 28	522 41	878 44	851 12	151 31
Kent,.......	4,935 48	1,036 32	2,289 82	1,242 30	366 04
Lapeer,.....	1,276 67	340 61	761 78	401 43	372 36
Lenawee,....	3,684 45	622 79	2,959 96	....	101 40
Livingston,...	2,185 72	269 23	1,684 32	49 69	192 45
Macomb,.....	1,890 71	464 59	788 69	356 33	281 16
Monroe,.....	4,806 98	1,275 05	1,992 17	1,431 93	107 83
Montcalm,....	867 56	80 60	162 19	443 28	181 40
Oakland,.....	1,558 74	265 07	1,081 88	114 04	97 75
Ottawa,.....	4,581 36	732 44	1,795 16	1,682 74	371 62
Saginaw,.....	3,175 16	386 24	1,075 80	1,393 56	319 56
Shiawassee,...	4,941 03	637 84	2,306 23	1,686 32	306 64
St. Clair,.....	2,973 11	354 11	1,766 17	542 28	310 55
St. Joseph,....	1,782 57	307 31	1,042 42	312 15	120 69
Sanilac,.....	1,159 19	50 28	763 99	222 71	122 21
Tuscola,.....	1,210 02	484 96	271 10	448 11	5 83
Van Buren,...	3,357 01	552 83	1,872 32	533 78	398 06
Washtenaw,...	1,433 78	117 79	1,242 02	40 02	33 95
Wayne,......	2,991 11	535 24	1,267 63	1,119 94	68 30
Total,.....	$99,695 60	$17,784 10	$52,986 11	$20,999 66	$7,925 72

[No. 6.]

Statement of Delinquent Taxes of 1852, returned to Auditor Genera'ls Office, and balances due to or from the several Counties, Nov. 30, 1853.

COUNTIES.	1852 Taxes return'd.	Dr. Nov. 30, 1853.	Cr. Nov. 30, 1853.
Allegan,	$7,958 28	$584 06	....
Barry,	6,534 92	222 37	....
Berrien,	6,266 34	4,396 59	....
Branch,	3,893 56	1,112 27	....
Calhoun	4,430 93	454 44	....
Cass	2,091 90	348 40	....
Chippewa	....	3,140 42	....
Clinton	6,485 11	....	20 80
Eaton	4,840 92	156 81	....
Genesee,	6,536 75	2,538 87	....
Hillsdale	6,095 40	1,658 84	....
Ingham,	6,127 20	....	594 22
Ionia,	5,168 73	467 22	....
Jackson,	2,811 38	5,416 83	....
Kalamazoo,	3,669 35	412 26	....
Kent,	7,370 03	4,002 68	....
Lapeer,	2,157 70	3,612 12	....
Lenawee	4,771 41	3,104 53	....
Livingston,	2,723 27	3,082 40	....
Mackinac,	....	643 22	....
Macomb,	2,220 06	4,066 10	....
Monroe	5,161 37	1,804 61	....
Montcalm	1.031 69	58 46	....
Oakland,	1,749 94	726 05	....
Ottawa	6,215 11	....	485 32
Saginaw	5,902 30	60	....
Shiawassee	7,433 89	....	4,758 81
St. Clair,	5,118 51	4,692 74	....
St. Joseph,	1,960 88	....	289 30
Sanilac	1,763 29	298 73	....
Tuscola	1,456 44	....	108 91
Van Buren,	5,810 96	8 32	....
Washtenaw,	1,129 27	12,291 91	....
Wayne	3,663 50	3,284 20	....
Total,	$140,549 89	$62,586 05	$6,257 36

[No. 7.]

Statement showing the Corporations paying Specific State Tax, the basis of their tax, the time when due, the time when paid, and the amounts paid during last fiscal year.

RAILROAD COMPANIES.

TITLE.	When tax due.	When tax paid.	Basis of Tax.	Rate per ct.	Amount of tax paid.
Michigan Central Railroad Company,	Jan. 31, 1853.	Feb. 3, '53, pt, Oct. 27, " bal.	$7,240,429 12	¾	$54,429 70
" Southern "	do	Feb. 11, " pt, Mar. 3, " bal.	3,061,974 14	¾	22,964 80
Erie & Kalamazoo "	do	Sept. 9, 1853.	319,863 39	½	1,597 31
Detroit & Pontiac "	Oct. 3, 1853.	Aug. 2, "	333,000 00	⅛	416 25
Chippewa Portage Company,		No report.		.....	

BANKS.

	When tax due.	When tax paid.	Basis of Tax.	Rate per ct.	Amount of tax paid.
Government Stock,	bal. due Jan. 31, 1852.	Dec. 31, 1852.	$198,000 00	1	$2,000 00
" "	" " 1853.	March 9, 1853.		1	1,000 00
Michigan Insurance Bank,	Jan. 10, "	Jan'y 16, "	230,483 60	1	2,000 10
Peninsular Bank,	"	Feb'y 22, "	1900 00	1	1,209 00
Farmer's & Mechanic's Bank,	"	March 2, "	100,000 00	1	1,000 00
Michigan State Bank,	April 1, "	April 8, "	151,578 00	¾	1,088 43
" "	Oct. 1, "	Oct. 31, "		¾	1,088 43

PLANK ROAD COMPANIES.

Jackson & Michigan,	July, 1851.	Dec. 10, 1852.		$138 90
"	" 1852.	" "		271 54
Plymouth & Dearborn,	" "	Dec. 29, 1852.		50 00
Monroe & Saline,	" "	" 31, "		?46 06
Walker & Vergennes,	" "	Jan'y 21, 1853.		2 50
Detroit and Birmingham,	" "	" 27, "		225 00
"	" 1853.	July 5, 1853.		240 00
Sant Ste Marie,	Feb, 1853.	" 5, "		10 10
Monroe & Erin,	July 1, 1853.	" 7, "		55 85

MINING COMPANIES.

Adventure,	Jan'y 1, 1853.	Dec. 17, 1852.	$48,228 05	1	$482 28
Albion,	July 1, "	" 20, 1853.	33,780 97	1	337 80
Algomah,	No report.				
Algonquin,					
Aztec,	Jan'y, "	Dec. 17, '52.	18,075 45	1	130 75
Bay State,	No report.				
Bluff,					
Bohemian,	July, 1853.	Nv. 7, 1853.	38,672 50	1	386 72
Boston,	No report.				
Cape,	Jan'y, 1853.	March 2, 1853.	22,906 00	1	229 06
Carp River,	No report.				
Cheesapeake,	Jan'y, 1853.	Jan'y 6, 1853.	24,200 00	1	242 00
Chippewa,	No report.				
Cleveland Iron,	July, 1853.	Aug. 24, 1853.	50 t's iron 10c p.t'n.		5 00

4

[No. 7.—Continued.]

MINING COMPANIES.

TITLE.	When tax due.	When tax paid.	Basis of tax.	Rate per ct.	Amount of tax paid.
Clifton,	No report.				
Copper Falls,	July, 1853.	July 1, 1853.	$46,204 00	1	$462 04
Copper Harbor,	No report.				
Cacique,	"				
Collins Iron,	"				
Continental,	"				
Cortez,	"				
Dana,	July, 1853.	Aug. 13, '53.	5 tons cop'r, $1	p. t'n.	5 00
Detroit & Lake Superior,	No report.				
Douglas Houghton,	Tax 1851, '52, and '53.	July, 1853. Nov. 9, 1853.	7,151 00	*1	220 53
Eagle Harbor,	"	July 7, "	7,131 89	1	71 32
Eagle River,	No report.				
Erie,	"				
Eureka,	Jan'y, 1853.	Jan'y 3, '53.	6,472 50	1	64 73
Evergreen Bluff,	No report.				
Empire,	"				
Fire Steel,	"				
Flint Steel River,	July, 1853.	Feb. 12, '58.	15 t's cop'r, $1	p. t'n.	15 00
Forrest,	"	July 1, '53.	43,478 81	1	434 79
Farm,	Feb'y, "	Dec. 2, '52.	12,500 00	1	125 00
Glen,	No report.				

Gogebec,	No report.				
Hungarian,	"				
Humbolt.	"				
Iron City,	July, 1853.	Jan'y 3, '53.	$36,216 50	1	$362 16
Isle Royal,	July, "	Nov. 12, '53.	27,907 68	1	279 07
Iron Mountain,	No report.				
Iroquois,	"				
Jackson,	"				
Keweenaw,	"				
Lac La Belle,	"				
Lake Superior,	"				
Lake Superior Iron,	"				
Lake Superior Fishing & Mining Co.,	"				
Lake Superior Mining Co. of Eagle Harbor,	"				
Mackinaw & Lake Superior,	"				
Magnetic,	"				
Meadow,	"				
Merchant,	"				
Michigan,	"				
Minnesota,	"				
Montezuma of Portage Lake,	July, 1853.	July 1, '53.	6,000 00	1	60 00
Native Copper,	No report.				
New England Iron,	July, 1853.	Nov. 22, '53.	22,254 58	1	222 54
New York & Michigan,	No report.				
Nebraska,	July, 1853.	July 5, '53.	149,835 50	1	1,498 35
North American,	No report.				
National,					

[No. 7.—Continued.]

MINING COMPANIES.

TITLE.	When tax due.	When tax paid.	Basis of tax.	Rate per ct.	Amount of tax paid.
North West Company of Michigan,	Jan'y '53.	Jan'y 7, '53.	$60,698 00	1	$606 98
North Western of Detroit,	July, '53.	Aug. 15, '53.	40,466 94	1	404 67
Ohio Trap Rock,	" "	July 5, '53.	57,356 64	1	573 56
Ontonagon, ...No report.					
Oriental "					
Ontario, "					
Pewabic. "					
Peninsular	Jan'y, '53.	Jan'y 10, '53.	29,290 00	1	292 90
Phenix,	July, "	July 1, '53.	21,484 91	1	214 85
Pittsburgh & Boston,	" "	June 18, "	110,905 00	1	1,109 05
Pittsburgh & Isle Royal,	" "	Nov. 10, "	25,546 25	1	260 77
Piscataqua, ...No report.					
Presque Isle, "					
Portage, "					
Quincy,	July, '53.	July 26, 53.	28,000 00	1	280 00
Ridge,	Jan'y, "	Jan'y 3, "	44,335 62	1	443 36
Ripley, ...No report.					
Rockland, "					
Shawmut, "					
Siskowit,	July, '53.	July 5, '53.	46,495 74	1	464 95
South East, ...No report.					

Star,	No report.				
Summit,	"	July, 1853.	July, 1853.	$10,000 00	$50 00
Swamscot,	No report.				
Shelden,	No report.				
Tolsio Consolidated,	July, 1853.	Aug. 13, 1853.	10t's cop'r $1 pr t,		10 00
Union,	No report.				
Winthrop,	"				
Ward,	"				

[No. 8.]

Statement of Acting Brokers—the amount of tax they pay, the amount of capital on which they pay, and the date of payment for the last fiscal year.

NAMES.	Capital.	When Tax paid.	Tax.
D. McIntyre,	$1,000 00	Dec'r 1, 1852.	15 00
Follett, Conklin & Co.,	600 00	" 12, "	9 00
Bidwell & Miles,	400 00	" 28, "	6 00
W. H. Waldby,	1,000 00	" 31, "	15 00
W. A. Butler,	2,000 00	Jan'y 8, 1853.	30 00
S. H. Ives & Co.,	2,000 00	" 14, "	30 00
C. T. Gorham,	500 00	" 20, "	7 50
Ransom & Dodge,	10,000 00	April 11, "	150 00
J. C. Bailey,	800 00	" 25, "	12 00
Crippen & Fiske,	500 00	" 26, "	7 50
Ives & Miles,	400 00	" " "	6 00
J. A. Weeks & Co.,	1,000 00	" 27, "	15 00
N. H. Wing & Co.,	2,000 00	Sept. 20, "	30 00
L. C. Kellogg,	500 00	Nov. 7, "	7 50
Howard, Smith & Co.,	5,000 00	" 15, "	75 00
Total,			$415 50

[No. 9.]

Statement showing population June 1, 1850—aggregate of Real and Personal Estate as equalized by Board for 1851—aggregate of Real and Personal Estate as assessed and equalized by Board of Supervisors for 1853—amount added or deducted by State Board—aggregate of Real and Personal Estate as equalized by State Board for 1853, and amount of State Tax apportioned to the several counties for 1852 and 1853.

COUNTIES.	Pop'l'n June 1, 1850.	Aggregate of R'l and Personal Estate as eq'r'd by State Board, 1851	Aggregate of R'l and Personal Estate as assessed by State Supervisors 1853	Aggregate of R'l and Per'n'l estate as eq'r'd by B'd 1853	Amount added or deducted by State Board.	Agg'te of R'l and Per'n'l estate as eq'r'd by State Board 1853	State Tax portioned 1852.	State Tax portioned 1853.	State Tax apportioned for 1853.
Allegan,	5,127	$488,677 99	1,541,737 43	1,541,737 43	Ded. $290,000 00	$1,341,737 43	$1,736		$111 47
Barry,	5,072	469,769 00	1,210,484 85	1,224,587 95		1,224,587 95	1,455		101 74
Berrien,	11,417	775,038 31	3,022,658 00	3,060,863 55		3,060,863 55	2,752		251 30
Branch,	12,472	837,289 15	3,138,308 00	2,874,334 00	Add 863,954 00	3,738,308 00	2,973		310 38
Calhoun,	19,169	1,637,347 00	3,742,270 00	3,646,946 00	" 1,783,758 00	5,430,704 00	5,814		451 20
Cass,	10,906	841,411 00	2,710,660 00	2,704,660 00	" 244,278 00	2,944,936 00	2,967		244 67
Clinton,	5,102	389,783 00	1,174,323 00	1,164,959 00		1,164,959 00	1,369		96 79
Chippewa,	898	105,291 00				209,000 00	373		16 68
Eaton,	7,058	519,614 52	1,699,927 00	1,732,854 00	Add 566,319 46	1,732,854 00	1,845		143 97
Genesee,	12,031	735,209 23	2,980,924 54	2,546,036 54	Ded. 157,702 76	3,114,356 00	3,610		259 76
Hillsdale,	16,159	993,240 00	4,169,523 76	4,167,525 76		4,009,523 00	3,527		333 19
Ingham,	8,597	568,367 00	1,870,153 00	1,853,069 00		1,853,069 00	2,069		163 96
Ionia,	7,597	515,993 67	1,938,130 50	2,007,218 87		2,007,218 87	1,632		166 76
Jackson,	19,433	1,516,459 01	5,758,013 00	5,723,798 00		4,723,798 00	6,386		476 55
Kalamazoo,	13,179	1,093,192 15	4,787,874 09	4,810,655 00		4,810,655 00	3,692		399 67
Kent,	12,017	883,014 78	3,734,440 00	3,562,823 00		3,562,823 00	3,135		396 80
Lapeer,	7,026	406,400 89	1,771,819 33	1,666,118 59		1,666,118 00	1,443		138 43
Livingston,	13,475	807,667 20	2,738,576 86	3,278,636 97	Ded. 300,000 00	3,076,636 97	2,866		255 78
Lenawee,	26,380	2,358,059 82	9,599,431 00	9,599,813 00		9,599,813 00	8,373		798 40
Mackinac,		197,709 70	169,902 70	169,902 25		169,902 25	453		14 11
Macomb,	15,532	896,246 00	4,366,399 00	4,510,399 00	Ded. 500,000 00	4,010,399 00	3,181		333 20
Monroe,	14,095	960,344 22	3,843,595 00	3,811,875 00		3,311,875 00	3,410		316 71
Montcalm,	894	109,182 55	963,422 00	291,645 00		291,645 00	287		24 93
Newaygo,			153,998 75	153,998 75		153,998 75			15 78
Oakland,	31,967	2,441,475 74	8,618,290 00	8,617,930 00		8,617,930 00	8,660		714 00
Ottawa,	5,587	451,847 23	1,239,114 25	1,322,479 70		1,322,479 70	1,711		109 88
Saginaw,	9,609	357,973 01	1,297,303 49	1,336,602 22		1,336,602 22	1,571		111 00
Shiawassee,	5,233	411,666 49	1,155,017 00	1,250,488 00		1,250,488 00	1,461		166 30

[No. 8.—Continued.]

COUNTIES.	Pop'l't'n June 1, 1850.	Aggregate of R'l and Person'l Estate as eq'l'z'd by State Board 1851.	Aggregate of R'l and Personal Estate as assessed by B'd 1853.	Agg'te of R'l and Person'l Estate as equal'z'd by State Supervisors 1853	Amount added or deducted by State Board.	Agg'te of R'l and Person'l Estate as equal'r'd by State Board 1853.	State Tax apportioned for 1852.	State Tax apportioned for 1853.
St. Clair,......	10,411	977,961 25	3,325,076 02	3,052,532 39	Add 826,511 61	3,909,044 00	3,470 36	394 78
St. Joseph,....	12,717	1,058,929 00	4,104,713 00	4,116,975 00	....	4,116,975 00	3,866 87	342 06
Sanilac,......	2,115	221,225 19	776,657 00	776,657 00	....	776,657 00	785 60	64 54
Tuscola,......	291	115,249 58	281,122 43	278,157 93	....	278,157 93	409 26	23 12
Van Buren,....	5,618	541,663 35	1,482,757 79	1,683,561 14	....	1,683,561 14	1,923 50	139 88
Washtenaw,...	28,569	2,517,457 00	9,012,392 00	9,375,000 00	....	9,375,000 00	8,939 66	778 88
Wayne,......	42,765	3,833,213 76	17,953,595 00	16,097,531 30	Add 2,856,193 70	18,953,595 00	13,612 16	1,574 67
Totals,.....	....	$30,976,370 18	$115,047,758 95	$114,049,162 34	....	$120,302,474 35	$116,000 00	$10,000 00

[No. 10.]

Ledger Balances on Auditor General's Books, Nov. 30, 1853.

	DR.	CR.
General Fund,		$254,997 21
Internal Improvement Fund,	$393,857 91	
University Fund,		73,504 46
University Interest Fund,		5,791 58
State Building Fund,	697 07	
Primary School Fund,		378,028 77
Primary School Interest Fund,		21,192 10
Normal School Fund,		2,706 81
Normal School Interest Fund,		3,380 91
Contingent Fund,		786 00
Asylum Fund,		12,716 22
Saut Ste Marie Canal Fund,	1,071 92	
Swamp Land Fund,	655 30	
Treasury Notes,		795 00
State Treasurer,	*375,625 70	
Michigan Central Railroad Deposits,		2,214 41
" Southern "		356 72
St. Joseph Valley		255 00
Land Warrants,		2,455 89
" (second series,)		7,436 28
Internal Improvement Warrants,		5,290 54
Total,	$771,907 90	$771,907 90

*To the above balance charged State Treasurer, is to be added $147 98 for outstanding Warrants, making actual cash balance in State Treasurer's hands, $375,773 68.

CIRCULARS TO SUPERVISORS.

AUDITOR GENERAL'S OFFICE,
Lansing, Mich., February 14, 1853.

By the Tax Law this day approved, you are required to assess *all property at its true value.* To arrive at its *true value,* you are to affix the price you would appraise it at in *payment of a just debt due from a solvent debtor.* Your attention is particularly directed to this provision—for if it be not faithfully and efficiently carried out, the object of the Legislature will be entirely defeated. The assessment of property at less than its true value, has become a great evil—it makes our *rate* of taxation extremely high, and deters emigration to our State. Under the new law, faithfully executed, there can be no doubt that the valuation of the State will reach $130,000,000, instead of some $30,000,-000, as at present. A State Board of Equalization being established, the State Tax is apportioned according to the valuation as fixed by them; consequently, there is no longer any inducement to make a low valuation for the purpose of avoiding a due proportion of the State Tax. Section 13 makes some explanations, to which you are referred.

Another important feature of the new law is, the *listing of all property* not exempt from taxation. The object of this is, to compel *all* to bear their due share of the burthens of taxation. It is well known that large amounts of personal property, moneys and credits under the old law, and in the possession of those most *able to pay,* entirely escaped taxation.

I am well aware that some inconvenience will arise in taking the first assessment under this law—but a liberal construction should be given to it, and an honest and earnest effort on the part of Supervisors to faithfully carry out its provisions, will result in much good. When a similar law was enacted in Ohio, an attempt was made in some cases, to *ridicule* it, by making a *minute list of all articles, &c.,* but the system has been sustained by the people, and has resulted in immense benefit to the State.

In making out the list, you should see that the property exempted is properly deducted. Opposite the 9th subdivision of section 15 of the list, you are to put down the amount of merchandize as appears from the inventory of the merchant. It is no hardship for the merchant to exhibit his inventory—for every good business man ought at least every year to make such inventory, and knowing when the law requires it, he can have it ready for the Supervisor when he calls to take the assessment.

For the purpose of appraisal and assessment, you are to deduct the amount in the 13th and 14th subdivisions from the amount in the 11th subdivision. Under the 12th subdivision, you are to include household furniture, &c., deducting the $200 worth, exempted by section 5, if not previously deducted.

If you believe that any person has attempted to conceal *any* of his property, or to so dispose of it as to avoid taxation, you can question any other person, under oath, as to that fact, that you may suppose has knowledge thereof.

There will be a meeting of the Board of Supervisors on the second Monday of June, 1853, to equalize, &c., as required by Act No. 106, of the Laws of 1851; and there will be a meeting of the State Board of Equalization on the 3d Monday of August of the same year, to which your Board can send delegates or not, as they may see fit.

Your attention is also particularly directed to section 18 of the act. Such an entire change in the system having been effected, it is of the utmost consequence, that each taxable inhabitant have the blank list, that ignorance of the law may not be plead as an excuse for not complying with it.

Should any one neglect or refuse to furnish you the list, you should, in addition to the fine of $25, as provided in section 19, use every exertion to bring out all the property of such delinquent, for the purpose of taxation.

There are undoubtedly many defects in the law, and should you at any time discover any that might seem to require legislative action, you will confer a favor by communicating with me upon the subject, that I may lay the same before the Legislature at its next biennial session.

JOHN SWEGLES,

Auditor General.

N. B. The amount of indebtedness may or may not be stated, at the option of the tax-payer; but cannot be deducted unless stated in some form, under oath. If the indebtedness equals or exceeds the amount of "moneys and credits," it is only necessary to state that fact, without giving the exact amount of such indebtedness, and the language of the two last lines of the affidavit may be varied so as to meet the case.

AUDITOR GENERAL'S OFFICE, }
Lansing, Mich., April 13, 1853. }

SIR:—As there appears to be some misapprehension in regard to a meeting of the Board of Supervisors in June next, I herewith append a copy of the act passed by the last Legislature:

[No. 97.]

AN ACT to provide for a meeting of the State Board of Equalization in Eighteen Hundred and Fifty-three.

SECTION 1. *The People of the State of Michigan enact,* That the State Board of Equalization be and they are hereby required to meet at the Capitol, in the village of Lansing, on the third Monday of August, in the year one thousand eight hundred and fifty-three, and after organizing as required by law, shall proceed to examine the tabular statements of the board of supervisors of each county, provided for in the fourth section of this act, and to hear the representatives from the several boards of supervisors as hereinafter provided, and they shall determine whether the relative valuation between the several counties is equal and uniform, according to location, soil, improvements, productions and manufactures; and also, whether the personal estate of the several counties has been uniformly estimated, according to the best information which can be derived from the statistics of the State, or from any other source.

Sec. 2. If, after such examination, such assessment shall be determined relatively unequal, they shall equalize the same by adding to or deducting from the aggregate valuation of taxable real and personal estate in such county or counties, such an amount as will produce relative equal and uniform valuations between the several counties in the State, and the amount added to or deducted from the valuation in each county shall be entered upon their records; and the valuations of the several counties, as equalized, shall be certified and signed by the Chairman and Secretary of the Board, and filed in the office of the Auditor General, and shall be the basis for apportioning all State taxes until another equalization shall be made.

Sec. 3. It shall be the duty of the Auditor General, as soon as may be after the determination of the State Board of Equalization shall be filed in his office, as provided in the preceding section, to send a certified transcript of the same to the treasurer of each county, who shall cause the same to be published in one or more papers in the county.

Sec. 4. A meeting of the board of supervisors for the year eighteen hundred and fifty-three, shall be held on the second Monday of June of said year; and when convened, the board shall proceed to equalise the assessment rolls, and their clerk shall certify and return such equalization to the Auditor General in the manner and at the time prescribed by the act establishing a State Board of Equalization, approved April seventh, eighteen hundred and fifty-one, except as herein otherwise provided.

Approved February 14, 1853.

THE NEW TAX LAW.

Although the principles of the new law *are precisely similar* to those of the old, many questions arise as to construction. This is because the new law in detail *compels* a full and proper compliance with the law *as it is and as it was*. The Supervisor of Pontiac, Oakland county, F. DARROW, Esq., has submitted to me the following interrogatories, and as they seem to meet nearly all the disputed points, not heretofore explained, I have concluded to answer them in this form:

1st. Must all demands which are doubtful be given in, as well as those which are good?

ANS. They must; but the Supervisor is to appraise them at their *cash value.*

2d. Where an individual has endorsed a note or become security by signing bond or contract, can it be deducted from his money and credits?

ANS. It cannot, until it is rendered certain that the surety will have to pay the amount of the bond or contract.

3d. Can demands, in the hands of lawyers or other persons for collection, be taxed, if the owner reside out of the State?

Ans. Any evidence of indebtness, owned out of the State and sent to some person in the State merely for collection, I think ought not to be taxed. But where agents are appointed in this State to loan money, sell land, &c., and to receive security therefor, and generally to transact all the business connected therewith, the amount of moneys, mortgages, notes, or other evidences of indebtedness held by such agent, should be taxed. See section 14 of the law.

4th. Must a person swear to his indebtedness, if he does not claim to have it deducted?

Ans. He need not; the last two lines of the form of oath on the statement may then be erased.

5th. Must an inventory be made *minutely* of property or merchandize, or can it be given in according to the best knowledge of the owner?

Ans. It is entirely optional with the Supervisor. The words "as per inventory" were placed in the blank to show that the Supervisor might *require* an inventory if he saw fit to do so.

6th. How are farmers to arrive at the number of bushels of grain, tons of hay and acres of cleared land?

Ans. Just as they have heretofore, and if the Supervisor thinks it is not correctly stated, he can require an exact measurement. In all cases the Supervisor should see that the exemptions are properly deducted.

7th. If the wife owns property, must the husband swear to it?

Ans. He must, if he hold it as such; if not the wife must swear to it.

8th. If the tax-payer is absent, must the wife swear to his property?

Ans. The Supervisor can examine any one under oath, in such cases, whom he may believe has knowledge of the amount or value of such property.

9th. How is the fine to be collected?

Ans. The same as other fines. The Prosecuting Attorney is to give his counsel and advice to Supervisors free of charge.

10th. Can blanks be left after 3d Monday?

Ans. They should be left before the third Monday of April. No person can be *compelled* to give in a list under oath if served after said third Monday, but the Supervisor must ascertain and appraise the property, according to the best of his ability.

11th. Can the Supervisor swear an individuul "*to the best of his knowledge and belief?*"

Ans. I cannot see how a person can swear beyond his "*knowledge and belief.*" It can make no difference whether those words are placed in the affidavit or not.

12th. If an individual reside here, and has money out of the State and not on interest, can it be taxed?

Ans. It can. See first clause of section 3.

In addition to the above, I would say, that the Town Board are to decide the *per cent.* to be paid to the Town Treasurer. The lists should be folded (as the samples heretofore forwarded) and placed in alphabetical order in the Supervisor's office for future reference.

I have said, that "the opposition to the new law comes from the *capitalists* of the State—those most able to bear taxation." For this I have been charged with endeavoring to create a prejudice against that class of our citizens. If an earnest and honest desire to compel *all* property to pay its just proportion of the burthens of taxation can be so construed, then am I guilty of the charge. No good citizen will attempt, by subterfuge or otherwise, to escape his just proportion of the expenses of the government which protects him. The person who will not *willingly* give in *all* his property for taxation, should be *compelled* to do so, in order that his neighbors may not be made to pay a portion of his tax.

JOHN SWEGLES,
Auditor General.

AUDITOR GENERAL'S OFFICE, }
Lansing, Mich., June 1, 1853. }

At a meeting of your Board on the second Monday of June, inst., you are required to "examine the assessment rolls of the several townships," and if the valuation of the real estate be relatively unequal, you are to "equalize the same." You can add to or deduct from the value of the real estate of any township, such an amount as will make such township relatively equal and uniform. There is no provision for equalizing *personal property*—the reason of this is, that its value cannot be so well determined by your Board, as by an individual Supervisor, who has examined each article; and although it is apparent that the great majority of Supervisors in the State have endeavored *honestly and faithfully* to carry out the spirit and intent of the new tax law, by assessing *all* property at its *true value*, yet there are, no doubt, a few cases in every county, where the Supervisor, fearing to get his town valued above the other towns, has adhered too closely to the *old custom* of assessing at *less* than its full value. You should add to the valuation of such towns a sum sufficient to make them *relatively equal* with the towns that are assessed at their *full value*.

The practice under the old law of assessing property at less than its true value, was, in too many cases, an effort of *one town to cheat another*—this practice is highly reprehensible—it injures the standing and credit of our State, and should be promptly and efficiently remedied by the action of your Board.

The State Board of Equalization meet in August next, and will take good care that no county, by a low valuation, shall escape a just proportion of the State tax—neither will any county, by a high valuation, be required to pay too much. It rests then, with your Boards to affix such a valuation as will truly and correctly exhibit the immense wealth of our young and growing State.

Some of those who were opposed to the law, have supposed they could refuse to comply with its requirements with impunity, because the law itself does not specify the mode and manner of collecting the penalty. Such persons are referred to section 1, chapter 128 of the revised statutes. Section 12 of the same chapter, points out the duty of the Supervisor.

At the time of transmitting to this office the assessed and equalized valuation of your county, any other information of the practical working of the new law will be thankfully received.

As I have previously stated, there are no doubt, many defects in the law—these can the more readily be discovered by a free interchange of views and opinions between the officers entrusted with its enforcement.

Very respectfully, &c.,
JOHN SWEGLES,
Auditor General.

STATE OF MICHIGAN.

1853.

DOCUMENT No. 2.

ANNUAL REPORT of the State Treasurer.

STATE TREASURER'S OFFICE, }
Lansing, Dec. 1, 1853. }

To His Excellency, ANDREW PARSONS, *acting Governor of the State of Michigan:*

SIR:—In accordance with the requirements of law, I have the honor to submit the following statements, showing the condition of the several funds, for the fiscal year ending Nov. 30th, 1853:

The balance in the Treasury on that date, was ($375,773 68,) Three Hundred and Seventy-five thousand Seven hundred and Seventy-three dollars and Sixty-eight cents.

By the terms of Act No. 63, of 1853, it was made my duty to require of any bank, before making it a depository of the surplus funds belonging to the State, good and ample security to be approved by the State Treasurer, Auditor General, and Secretary of State, for the safe keeping and reimbursement of said funds, when called for, and the payment of interest thereon, at the rate of not less than one per cent. per annum. The only banks or persons which proposed to file the security above required, were the Michigan Insurance Bank and the Peninsular Bank of Detroit, and their proposition was to pay one per cent. only. As these were the *only* offers I received, or ever have received, I closed with them, and they have been the depositories of the surplus funds for the past year, at the rate of one per cent. per annum.

1

I have reason to suppose that a more favorable arrangement can be made for the ensuing year, and at a higher rate of interest. As the law does not divest me of responsibility for the *safe keeping* of the public funds, I trust I shall not be censured for making their safety and security a principal object in my selection of depositaries.

I also submit herewith the annual statements of the several banks in this State at the time of my annual examination of them.

All of which is respectfully submitted.

B. C. WHITTEMORE,
State Treasurer.

Treasurer of the State of Michigan in account with the State of Michigan.

DR.

1853.

Nov. 30.	To balance in Treasury, Nov. 30, 1852,......			$116,555	21
"	" receipts on account of General fund,.......			373,515	51
"	"	"	"	Int. Imp. "	74,952	14
"	"	"	"	Primary School fund,	107,417	20
"	"	"	"	University fund,.....	34,984	44
"	"	"	"	Pri. School Int. fund,	43,664	65
"	"	"	"	University Int. "	11,287	97
"	"	"	"	State Building "	2,651	21
"	"	"	"	Asylum "	1,710	91
"	"	"	"	Nor. Sch. endow. "	3,909	79
"	"	"	"	" " Int. "	1,319	04
"	"	"	"	St. Jo. Val. R. R. Dep.	255	00

Total,_____ $772,223 07

CR.

Nov. 30.	By am't paid out on acc't of General fund,....		$205,833	12
"	"	"	Internal Improvement "	112,403	92
"	"	"	Primary School Int. "	54,517	06
"	"	"	University Interest "	15,105	45
"	"	"	Contingent	214	00
"	"	"	Asylum -	1,993	49
"	"	"	Normal School Endow. "	1,479	57
"	"	"	" " Int. "	3,781	38
"	"	"	Treasury Notes,............	1	00
"	"	"	Swamp Land fund,.........	2	80
"	"	"	Sault Ste. Marie Canal fund,..	1,071	92
"	"	"	Mich. South. R. R. deposits,...	15	00
"	"	"	Mich. Central R. R. deposits,..	80	68
"	" balance in Treasury, Nov. 30, 1853,......		375,773	68

Total,_____ $772,223 07

Ledger Balances, November 30, 1858.

DR.

1853.

Nov. 30.	Cash,	$375,773	68
"	Internal Improvement fund,	378,675	20
"	Swamp Land fund,	655	30
"	Sault Ste. Marie Canal fund,	1,071	92
"	State Building fund,	697	07
Total,		$756,873	17

CR.

Nov. 30.	General fund,	$255,044	94
"	Primary School fund,	378,028	77
"	Primary School interest fund,	21,292	35
"	University fund,	73,504	46
"	University interest fund,	5,791	58
"	Contingent fund,	786	00
"	Asylum fund,	12,716	22
"	Normal School fund,	2,706	81
"	Normal School interest fund,	3,380	91
"	Treasury Notes,	795	00
"	Mich. Central R. R. deposits,	2,214	41
"	Mich. South. R. R. deposits,	356	72
"	St. Jo. Valley R. R. deposits,	255	00
Total,		$756,873	17

GENERAL FUND.

DR.

1853.

Nov. 30. To warrants paid during fiscal year,.............$905,863 12
"   amount transferred to University Int. Fund, 8,651 79
"   "   Internal Imp.   "   75,000 00
"   "   Contingent   "   3,000 00
"   Nor. Schl. Int. "   5,012 72
                     Primary School "   21,532 63
"   "   Asylum   "   13,000 00
"   balance Nov. 30, 1853,................ 255,044 94

Total,..$587,075 20

CR.

Nov. 30. By balance Nov. 30, 1852,................$201,687 08
"   receipts during fiscal year,................ 373,515 51
              amount transferred from Contingent fund,.. 11,872 61

Total,..$587,075 20

INTERNAL IMPROVEMENT FUND.

DR.

1853.

Nov. 30. To balance Nov. 30, 1852,...............$416,223 42
"   warrants paid during fiscal year,......... 112,403 92

Total,..$528,627 34

CR.

Nov. 30. By receipts during fiscal year,...............$74,952 14
"   amount transferred from General fund,...... 75,000 00
"   balance Nov. 30, 1853,................378,675 20

Total,..$528,627 34

PRIMARY SCHOOL FUND.
DR.

1853.

Nov. 30. To balance Nov. 30, 1853,.................\$378,028 77

Total,..\$378,028 77

CR.

Nov. 30. By balance Nov. 30, 1852,................\$270,611 57
"   receipts during fiscal year,............... 107,417 20

Total,..\$378,028 77

UNIVERSITY FUND.

1853.

Nov. 30. To balance Nov. 30, 1853,................\$73,504 46

Total,..\$73,504 46

CR.

Nov. 30. By balance Nov. 30, 1852,................\$38,520 02
"   receipts during fiscal year,............... 34,984 44

Total,..\$73,504 46

ASYLUM FUND.
DR.

1853.

Nov. 30. To balance Nov. 30, 1852,................   \$1 20
"   warrants paid during fiscal year,..........   1,993 49
        balance Nov. 30, 1853,.................. 12,716 22

Total,.. \$14,710 91

CR.

Nov. 30. By amount receipts during fiscal year,......... \$1,710 91
"   "   transferred from General fund,..... 13,000 00

Total,.. \$14,710 91

NORMAL SCHOOL ENDOWMENT FUND.

DR.

1853.

Nov. 30. To warrants paid during fiscal year,..............$1,479 57

"   balance Nov. 30, 1853,.................... 2,706 81

Total,..$4,186 38

CR,

Nov. 30. By balance Nov. 30, 1852,.................. $276 59

"   amount transferred from Nor. Sch. Int. fund, 2,224 70

receipts during fiscal year,................ 1,685 09

Total,..$4,186 38

NORMAL SCHOOL INTEREST FUND.

DR.

1853.

Nov. 30. To warrants paid during fiscal year,............$1,506 68

"   amount transferred to Nor. Sch. End. Fund,.. 2,224 70

balance Nov. 30, 1853,.................... 3,380 91

Total,..$7,112 29

CR.

Nov. 30. By balance Nov. 30, 1852,.................. $780 53

"   receipts during fiscal year,................ 1,319 04

-      amount transferred from General fund,..... 5,012 72

Total,..$7,112 29

MICHIGAN SOUTHERN RAILROAD COMPANY DEPOSITS.

DR.

1853.

Nov. 30. To warrants paid during fiscal year,...........	$15 00
" balance Nov. 30, 1853,...................	356 72
Total,...	$371 72

CR.

Nov. 30. By balance Nov. 30, 1852,...................	$371 72
Total,...	$371 72

SWAMP LAND FUND.

DR.

1853.

Nov. 30. To balance Nov. 30, 1852,..................	$652 51
" warrants paid during fiscal year,...........	2 80
Total,...	$655 30

CR.

Nov. 30. By balance Nov. 30, 1853,...................	$655 30
Total,...	$655 30

PRIMARY SCHOOL INTEREST FUND.

DR.

1853.

Nov. 30. To warrants paid during fiscal year,..........	$54,517 06
" balance Nov. 30, 1853,...................	21,292 35
Total,...	$75,809 41

CR.

Nov. 30. By balance Nov. 30, 1852,..................	$10,612 13
" receipts during fiscal year,................	43,664 65
" amount transferred from General fund,......	21,532 63
Total,...	$75,809 41

UNIVERSITY INTEREST FUND.
DR.

1853.

Nov. 30.	To warrants paid during fiscal year,..........	$15,105 45
"	balance Nov. 30, 1853,..............	5,791 58
	Total,.......................................	$20,897 03

CR.

Nov. 30.	By balance Nov. 30, 1852,..............	$957 27
"	receipts during fiscal year,.............	11,287 97
"	amount transferred from General fund,.....	8,651 79
	Total,.......................................	$20,897 03

CONTINGENT FUND.
DR.

1853.

Nov. 30.	To warrants paid during fiscal year,..........	$214 00
"	amount transferred to General fund per Joint Resolution, No. 15, 1853,..............	11,872 61
"	balance Nov. 30, 1853,..............	786 00
	Total,.......................................	$12,872 61

CR.

Nov. 30.	By balance Nov. 30, 1852,..............	$9,872 61
"	transferred from General fund,...........	3,000 00
	Total,.......................................	$12,872 61

MICHIGAN CENTRAL RAILROAD COMPANY DEPOSITS.

DR.

1853.

Nov. 30. To warrants paid during fiscal year, ...   80 86
   "   balance Nov. 30, 1853, ... 2,214 41

Total, ...$2,295 09

CR.

Nov. 30. By balance Nov. 30, 1852, ...$2,295 09

Total, ...$2,295 09

STATE BUILDING FUND.

DR.

1853.

Nov. 30. To balance Nov. 30, 1852, ...$3,348 28

Total, ...$3,348 28

CR.

Nov. 30. By receipts during fiscal year, ...$2,651 21
   "   balance Nov. 30, 1853, ...   697 07

Total, ...$3,348 28

ST. JOSEPH VALLEY RAILROAD COMPANY'S DEPOSITS.

DR,

1853.

Nov. 30. To balance Nov. 30, 1853, ...$255 00

Total, ... : $255 00

CR.

Nov. 30. By receipts during fiscal year, ...$255 00

Total, ...$255 00

SAULT STE. MARIE CANAL FUND.

DR.

1853.

Nov. 30. To warrants paid during fiscal year,............$1,071 92

Total,...$1,071 92

CR.

Nov. 30. By balance Nov. 30, 1853,...................1,071 92

Total,...$1,071 92

Statement showing the condition of all the Banks in this State at the time the following Reports were made.

Statement of the condition of the Bank of Macomb County, Monday, January 2d, 1854.

RESOURCES.

Due from Banks and Bankers,..................		$226,583 28
Foreign Bills of Exchange,..................		254,182 76
Domestic Bills,..................		44,369 25
Cash—Coin,..................	$76,331 23	
" Notes of other Banks,..........	23,137 25	
" Cash Items,..................	1,104 85	
" Checks on other Banks,..........	5,000 00	
		105,573 33
Real Estate,..................		5,450 00
Bank Furniture, Plates, &c.,..................		1,969 46
Personal Property,..................		700 00
Expenses,..................		6,126 92
Total,..................		$644,955 00

LIABILITIES.

Capital Stock,..................	$250,000 00
Due Depositors,..................	10,044 00
Notes in Circulation,..................	384,911 00
Total,..................	$644,955 00

James G. Tucker, Cashier of the Bank of Macomb County, being duly sworn, says that the above statement of the condition of said Bank is true, to the best of his knowledge and belief.

J. G. TUCKER, *Cashier.*

Subscribed and sworn this third day of January, 1854, before me,

JNO. STOCKTON, *J. P.*

Statement showing the condition of the Government Stock Bank on the morning of Dec. 30, 1853.

RESOURCES.

*United States stocks deposited with State Treasurer as security for circulating notes,		$130,800 00
Loans and discounts,		87,385 75
Due from banks and bankers on demand,		47,177 25
Cash on hand, viz:		
" Gold and silver coin,	$25,006 12	
" Bank notes,	11,009 00	
" Checks and drafts,	1,427 52	
		37,442 64
Michigan State Bonds,		1,000 00
Michigan University warrants,		3,766 65
Contingent account,		1,000 00
Expense account,		2,445 38
Plates and bills,		1,625 00
Furniture and fixtures,		493 47
Stock in Metropolitan Bank,		110 75
Total,		$313,246 89

LIABILITIES.

Capital stock,	$100,000 00
Countersigned circulating notes rec'd from State Treasurer in circulation,	130,800 00
Due to banks and bankers on demand,	27,000 00
Due depositors on demand,	46,116 03
Profits,	9,830 86
Total,	$313,246 89

---

* The amount of stocks deposited by this bank is $190,000. 9 per cent. premium is allowed the bank on them, and for which they have circulating notes. The bank is allowed by its charter to have circulating notes corresponding to the market value of the stocks in New York city.   STATE TREASURER.

State of *Michigan, Washtenaw Co., ss.*

Edwin R. Tremain, President of the Government Stock Bank, being duly sworn, doth depose and say, that the foregoing is a just and true statement of the condition of said bank, on the morning of December 30, 1853, according to the best of his knowledge and belief.

E. R. TREMAIN.

Sworn to and subscribed before me, this 31st day of December, A. D. 1853.

B. C. WHITTEMORE,
State Treasurer.

Condition of the Michigan State Bank, December 30, 1853.

Bills discounted,	$357,991	01
State Bonds, value,	10,000	00
Mich. Cent. Railroad 8 ⅌ ct. Bonds,	37,350	00
Ohio Junction, do	3,500	00
Real Estate, value,	6,000	00
Bonds and Mortgages,	18,937	18
Office Furniture, Safes, &c.,	1,312	28
Cash—Coin, ... $104,841 82		
" Bank Notes and Checks, ... 21,742 00		
" Banks, ... 140,491 98		
	267,075	80
Total,	$702,166	27

Capital Stock,	$151,678	00
Deposites,	168,355	71
Circulation,	350,867	00
Banks and Bankers,	2,802	91
Surplus Profits,	28,462	65
Total,	$702,166	27

State of Michigan, ss.

Before me, B. C. Whittemore, Treasurer of the State of Michigan, personally came Alexander H. Adams, Cashier of the Michigan State

Bank, who being duly sworn, deposeth and saith, that the above statement is true, according to the best of his knowledge and belief.

A. H. ADAMS, *Cashier.*

Subscribed and sworn to, this 30th day of December, 1853.

B. C. WHITTEMORE,

State Treasurer.

---

*Statement of the condition of the Farmers' and Mechanics' Bank
of Michigan, December 31st, 1853.*

RESOURCES.

Bills discounted, and other loans,	$342,183	43
Real Estate,	129,720	85
Bonds and Mortgages,	41,646	00
Land Contracts,	8,040	18
Bills of Exchange,	54,133	79
Judgments,	16,283	04
Stocks,	16,300	00
Personal Property,	3,571	75
Suspended Claims,	15,494	14
State Stocks,	102,119	38
Due from Banks and Agents,	21,304	18
" City of Detroit,	1,605	00
" sundry individuals,	15,491	76
Bank Notes and Checks,	1,300	73
Items counted as Cash,	1,548	69
Coin	5,093	05
Total,	$775,835	97

LIABILITIES.

Loans on time,	$178,783	42
Due stockholders for advancing 65 per ct.,	181,790	62
Special deposits applicable to debts due the Bank,	84,934	74
Due Banks,	2,751	34
" for collections,	1,309	06
" depositors,	12,376	39
Unpaid dividends,	295	00
" certificates,	5,465	36
Circulation,	74,270	50

Suspended accounts,	416	86
Excess of resources,	233,442	68
Total,	$775,835	97

State of Michigan, Wayne County, ss.

J. C. W. Seymour, Cashier of the Farmers' and Mechanics' Bank of Michigan, being duly sworn, deposes and says, that the above is a statement of the condition of said Bank on the 31st day of December, 1853, as appears from the books of said Bank.

JNO. S. VAN ALSTYNE,
Notary Public, Wayne Co., Mich..

Statement of the condition of the Peninsular Bank, Dec. 31, 1853.

RESOURCES.

Due from banks and bankers,	$100,313	93		
Bills in transit,	350	00		
			$100,663	93
Cash—Gold and silver,	31,795	03		
" Notes of other banks and checks,	22,824	00		
" Cash items,	1,630	18		
			56,249	21
Foreign bills of exchange,			293,069	01
Domestic bills,			180,669	98
Due from others, not included in the above,			3,414	52
Michigan bonds and warrants and U. S. land warrants,			17,855	65
State bonds deposited with State Treasurer,			128,068	19
Expense account,			1,328	00
Personal property,			4,407	14
Contingent account,			3,522	58
Total,			$789,248	21

LIABILITIES.

Due depositors,			$434,702	35
Due other banks,			7,823	03
Circulation,	$127,900	00		
Less this amount on hand,	3,849	00		
			124,051	00
Profit and loss,			21,421	83
Capital stock,			201,250	00
Total,			$789,248	21

State of Michigan, Wayne County, ss.

Henry H. Brown, being duly sworn, saith the above statement is true according to the best of his knowledge and belief.

H. H. BROWN, *Cashier.*

Sworn and subscribed before me, this 31st day of December, A. D. 1853.   B. C. WHITTEMORE, *State Treasurer.*

Statement of the Michigan Insurance Company Bank, Detroit, Jan. 1, 1854.

RESOURCES.

Cash—Gold coin,................$101,112 83	
" Silver " 13,495 20	
" Notes of solvent banks,........ 28,929 00	
" Checks on banks and bankers,... 20,030 63	
	$163,567 66
Bills discounted,....................	503,756 63
Bonds and mortgages,................	17,428 98
Real estate,........................	3,828 40
Due from banks and bankers,...........	180,168 02
Bank and railroad stocks,.............	29,706 25
Michigan State stocks in hands of State Treasurer,....	170,683 60
Office furniture,....................	2,556 15
Total,..........................	$1,071,695 69

LIABILITIES.

Capital Stock,.....................	$200,010 00
Profits,...........................	51,758 92
Office Notes, individual liability,........$119,992 00	
Stock notes,................... 159,090 00	
	$279.082 00
Less office notes on hand,............ 72,992 00	
	$206,090 00
Due banks and bankers,................	40,811 46
Due Board of Water Commissioners, City of Detroit,..	174,771 58
Due depositors,......................	398,253 73
Total,..........................	$1,071,695 69

State of Michigan, Wayne County, ss.

Henry K. Sanger, being duly sworn, says the above statement exhibits the true condition of the Michigan Insurance Company Bank, according to the best of his knowledge and belief.

H. K. SANGER, *Cashier.*

Sworn and subscribed before me, this 2d day of January, 1854.

W L. WHIPPLE,
Notary Public, Wayne Co., Mich.

STATE OF MICHIGAN.

1853.

DOCUMENT No. 3.

ANNUAL REPORT of the Board of State Auditors.

Office of the Secretary of State,
Lansing, Mich., Dec. 1, 1853.

To His Excellency, Andrew Parsons, *Governor of the State of Michigan:*

Sir—In compliance with the requirements of law, the undersigned respectfully submit the following report, showing the proceedings of the Board of State Auditors for the fiscal year ending Nov. 30, 1853:

On the first day of December, 1852, the Board examined the accounts of Bernard C. Whittemore, State Treasurer, and found that at the close of the fiscal year last past, he had on hand in cash, the sum of one hundred and sixteen thousand five hundred and fifty-five dollars and twenty-one cents, ($116,555 21,) which sum being exhibited to us as on hand in the State Treasury, was by us examined, and found correct.

PORTER KIBBEE,
Commissioner State Land Office.
JOHN SWEGLES,
Auditor General.

1

January 10, 1853. This day the Board had under consideration the claim of John Prentiss, for work done on the Northern Railroad, under a contract entered into by the State with Thomas J. Drake, and which contract was assigned by said Drake to said Prentiss. Upon a careful examination of all the documents, proofs, and the witnesses who were introduced by the claimant, the claim was rejected for the reason that the Board of Auditors on the 10th day of August, A. D. 1847, did examine all the proofs, and decided to reject this same claim.

January 12. The claim of Samuel W. Pitts, referred to the Board by act No. 110 of the session laws of 1851, for damages in consequence of the Southern Railroad crossing the land of said Pitts, was considered, and upon proof presented, was allowed at $50 00.

February 5. The Board had under consideration the claim of Anselom Arnold, for services and expenses in going to the State of New York, upon the requisition of Governor John S. Barry, issued September 30, 1850, upon the Governor of the State of New York, for the arrest of Azor H. Dayton, a fugitive from justice from the State of Michigan. The claimant files in support of his claim a copy of an indictment found against said Dayton at the October term of the Circuit Court of the County of Branch: also, journal of said Court showing his conviction: also, affidavit of Rufus Beals, Anselom Arnold, and E. G. Parsons, and upon the evidence here submitted, the claim was allowed at $140 25.

February 7. The claim of Governor Robert McClelland for balance of salary for the year 1852, was considered and allowed at $500 00.

February 12. The claim of William Megiveron, asking for extra compensation upon contract for planking side walks on Washington Avenue, in the town of Lansing, was rejected.

February 14. The Board had under consideration the claim of T. Barron, for extra services as Door Keeper of the House of Representatives, and of M. Goodrich for extra compensation as Messenger to the House of Representatives, which were rejected.

April 21. Board rejected the claims of D. C. Holbrook, and William T. Young, for services recording rules of Court &c., for the reason that they can find no authority of law for paying such accounts out of the State Treasury.

May 18. This day the petition of Mark Norris and others, to be relieved from certain liabilities incurred as sureties for Ypsilanti and Tecumseh Rail Road Company, referred to Board of Auditors, under Joint Resolution No. 11 of 1853, approved January 29, 1853, was taken up, and evidence satisfactory to the Board having been produced, it was unanimously decided to grant the relief asked for. Whereupon, the Board executed a release of certain mortgages, in accordance with the prayer of the petitioners.

The claims of Henry B. Miller, for printing delinquent tax sales for 1845; of J. Van Rensselaer, Clerk of Wayne County; E. B. Warner, Clerk of Cass County; and J. McMahon, Clerk of Washtenaw County, for services as clerks of Board of County Canvassers, making returns and recording the same, were rejected. The Board found no law authorizing the payment of such claims from the State Treasury.

The claim of W. S. Driggs, for damages, in consequence of building Clinton and Kalamazoo Canal, was rejected, for reason that claimant was not owner of the property at the time, nor for some years thereafter.

May 20. The claim of E. M. Pitcher, for one month and eighteen days services as First Lieutenant of Michigan Volunteers, previous to being mustered into the service of the United States, was allowed at $111 08.

July 7. In accordance with the following resolution of the Board of Auditors, R. R. Gibson was appointed by the Chairman, Secretary of said Board: "*Resolved*, That the Chairman of the Board of State Auditors be authorized to procure the services of a Secretary, whose duty it shall be to correctly keep and record the proceedings of this Board, and do such other duties as the Board may direct."

Nov. 29. On this day the Board had under consideration the following claim:

John F. Hamlin *vs.* State of Michigan—Claim for damages in consequence of suspension by State of work on section 16, Clinton and Kalamazoo Canal: Claimant, by his attorney Morgan L. Drake, Esq., files in support of his claim, affidavits of Joshua B. Taylor, Thomas J. Hunt, Charles W. Millerd, and C. W. Chapell; also, letters of Hon. Wm. A. Fletcher, Hon. Chas. W. Whipple, A. Turner, A. H. Adams, Peter Morey, and Amos Mead; also, legal questions decided by the Circuit Court in the case of Beach and Robinson *vs.* State of Michigan;

a like statement of James B. Hunt and O. D. Richardson, of the question decided in the Shiawassee Circuit, in the case of Williams and Williams *vs.* The State of Michigan. After hearing the argument of claimant's counsel, Morgan L. Drake, Esq., and a careful examination of all the testimony here presented, as well as the law touching the case, the Board unanimously decided to allow the claim at $2,500.

WM. GRAVES,

Chairman Board State Auditors.

List of claims allowed by the Board from December 1st, 1852, to November 30th, 1853, inclusive.

Dec. 31, 1852.

Geo. W. Peck, for advertising official canvass, 1852,		$62 10
"	binding 500 copies joint documents,	125 00
"	making 25 book cases, State Library,	12 50
"	advertising school lands, and printing for Land Office,	8 75
"	printing and binding for Auditor General's Office,	237 53
"	folding and pressing joint documents,	57 00
C. J. Fox, expenses incurred in State business,		15 00
Peter Low, services as senatorial canvasser,		4 75
Hoyt G. Post, " "		1 50
Wm. Beach,		3 00
Eli P. Watson,		10 50
L. Palmer,		2 00
Asa A. Scott,		25 00
Wm. N. Angel,		1 50
W. P. Beach,		1 50
E. F. Wade,		16 00
R. R. Gibson, extra services in Secretary of State's Office,		50 00
Geo. W. Perry, stationery furnished House of Representatives in 1850,		22 82

Wm. Langhorn, services as porter,.........................$201 00

John Stockton, services as Presidential Elector,............ 45 00

Wm. McCauley,   "   " 18 00

A. Edwards, ... 36 00

D. J. Campau, ... 51 00

Jno. S. Barry, ... 48 00

Salmon Sharp,   - 30 00

H. C. Everitt, straw for Capitol,......................... 1 25

V. S. Murphy, special messenger to procure Oakland Co. election returns,... 19 50

B. F. Bush, stationery,.................................. 6 75

J. P. Baker, painting Capitol building,................... 581 87

John Lynch, sawing wood,................................ 3 75

John Nelson, teaming,................................... 1 00

Smith & Cowles, tinning cupola, and nails,............... 114 22

Francis Foster, grubbing stumps in Capitol yard,.......... 3 00

Wm. Megiveron, clearing under act 133 of 1851,.......... 142 00

S. Dearin, setting trees in Capitol yard,................. 12 00

A. English, clearing on Mich. Avenue, 1849,............. 10 00

J. Barnes, bill of advertising,.......................... 171 60

S. W. Wright, sundry bills for State offices,............. 62 05

J. Page, lumber for Capitol,.......................... 20 00

H. Moots, repairs,.................................... 1 06

J. C. Fargo, express charges,.......................... 5 75

Stephens & Field, 1 box glass,......................... 3 75

J. A. Bailey, press for Land Office,.................... 24 00

L. Beecher & Co., carpeting for Capitol,............... 411 76

C. P. Woodward, stoves,.............................. 9 00

Duncklee, Wales & Co., advertising,................... 45 60

C. H. Taylor, pens for Sec. State's office,............. 5 50

Wm. Megiveron, lumber,.............................. 2 43

Humphrey & Hibbard, transportation,................. 1 88

C. Wakenhut, assisting porter,....................... 1 50

D. Dunckill, lime for Capitol,....................... 3 50

State Treasurer, counterfeit detector,................ 2 00

John Jennings, clearing on school section,............. 13 06

C. J. Fox, for expenses incurred in purchasing books for State
    Library, and other State business,................... .... $95 00

John Swegles, board of porter,.......... .... 19 50

Charles P. Bush, services and expenses locating lands for St.
    Marie Canal,.... ... . 170 09

Jan. 4, 1853.

C. C. Wood, for cushions for Senate Chamber,............ 135 00

W. Megiveron, repairs on bridge,.... .... 687 89

      "   extra services,.... .... 151 67

C. Wakenhut, sawing wood,....................... .... 89 00

R. McClelland, telegraphing and expenses,.... .... 6 28

Jan. 5, 1853.

H. L. & H. Baker, for making, painting, varnishing, and re-
    pairing chairs for Senate and House,.... .... 101 04

Jan. 12, 1853.

Hawks & Bassett, printing notice of general election, 1852,... 21 60

Jan. 21, 1853.

V. S. Murphy, services as librarian,.................... .... 45 00

Feb. 4, 1853.

D. G. McClure, keg white lead,.... .... 2 13

A. F. Weller, 15 days services copying and condensing school
    inspectors reports,.... .... 25 00

Mrs. Morehouse, work of self and daughter on carpets for Cap-
    itol, 10 days,.... .... 10 00

P. J. Loranger, services copying message, &c.,.... .... 31 00

Phelps & Stevens, for advertising Supreme and Circuit Court
    rules,.... ....'.... .... 9 80

A. D. Shaw, services as district canvasser,.... .... 1 50

J. H. Adams,   "   " 9 50

T. D. Green,   "   ' 3 70

C. C. Wood, bill of upholstering,.... .... 23 25

Mary Elliot, making carpet for capitol,.... .... 6 50

February 11, 1853.

Dr. Rudolph, for re-translation of the Governor's message into
    the French and German languages, and printing same,
    and sending to capitol,.... .... :.... .... 175 00

Edward Kanler, translating Governor's message into German, $50 00
E. N. Lacroix,   "   "   "   " French,   50 00
Detroit Free Press, paper,........... ....   7 50
Burgher & Dix, plat of Senate and House of Representatives,. 41 00
C. Piquette, pens for Secretary of State's office,........ .... 7 50
F. W. Shearman, traveling expenses,.............. ....   53 00
Humphrey & Hibbard, transportation,.... ....   1 75
G. & C. Merriam, Webster's Dictionary,................   24 00

February 12, 1853.
Israel Gillett, work about capitol,........................   88 43
Francis Otteny, services as porter,......................   14 00
Mrs. Harrison, washing,................................   4 06
B. F. Bush, notarial wafers for Secretary of State's Office,....   5 85
  "   stationery, and bill of stoves and spittoons,...... .. 102 36
A. E. Hathon, surveying,.......... ....   49 50
J. H. Lund, printing paper,........ ....   387 00
E. B. Danforth, transportation of oil cloth,...............   8 00
State Treasurer, pass book,....................../........   50
D. L. Case, expenses to Detroit and back for State,..........   10 25
Humphrey & Hibbard, transportation,....................   11 23
J. P. Baker, cutting, making, and putting down carpet,.....   6 00
Thompson & Godley, livery to Jackson,.... ....   8 00
Charles S. Hunt, services in Executive office,..............   15 00
John Whiteley, transportation,.........................   3 50
Mrs. Lillis, washing,................................   1 75
C. Wakenhut, sawing wood,............................   1 50
V. S. Murphy, services and livery,.... ....   29 00
W. Megiveron,   "   lumber,......................   24 15
J. C. Bailey, expenses to Detroit, for State,........ ....   15 00
E. D. Burr, services district canvasser,...................   2 75
L. Beecher & Co., carpeting,........ ....   72 00
Henry Hotailing, drawing sand,.............. ....   2 00
State Treasurer, gold pens for office,....................   7 75
C. Miller, 7¼ days services, cleaning and putting down carpets,
   Senate and House,..... ....   7 50
H. Gibbs, butts and screws,...........................   1 00
McClure & Ballard, thread for carpets,................. ....   1 16

Francis Otteny, 12½ days services,...................... $12 50

E. E. Beebee, bill of sundries for offices,............. ..... 12 18

V. S. Murphy, 12 days work on records in office of Sec. of

State,.. .... 16 90

Simpson & Pease, candles,............................... 31 51

Holmes & Co., velvet for Senate,...................... 21 87

Francis Otteny, 6 days work in Senate Chamber,.......... 6 00

H. B. Shank, 12 lbs. candles,.......... .... 6 00

John Farmer, copy map of Mich., on rollers,............. 6 00

Smith & Cowles, ewer, basin, tumblers, &c.,............. 6 63

E. B. Danforth, transportation,...................,..... 5 00

A. S. Bagg, letter book,................................ 2 25

Lyman Beecher & Co., carpet and making, H. of R.,....... 153 85

Guile & Allison, pen nibs for Land Office,............. 2 00

Thomas Gallagher, candles,............................. 158 82

Levi Hunt, bill of nails, &c.,......................... 31 98

Geo. Doty, clock for Senate chamber,................... 8 00

P. McKernan, services clerk Supreme Court, Lansing,...... 10 68

B. F. Bush, stationery for Superintendent of Public Instruction, 17 19

Francis Otteny, 7 days services,...................... 7 00

B. F. Bush, bill of stationery for Supreme Court,........... 11 00

John Farmer, 1 map for Treasurer's office,............. 6 00

R. B. Gilson, portraits of Washington and Jackson for State

Library,... 15 50

D. W. Buck, repairs on furniture in Capitol, and new work for

same,.. 297 17

February 14, 1853.

H. H. Brown, 4 days' attendance before committee of Senate,

and 170 miles travel,................................. 29 00

D. V. Bell, Jr., preparing Manual of 1853 for publication,.... 10 00

A. J. Graham, making chart of House of Representatives,.... 3 00

D. Chidester, services as district canvasser for County of Mack-

inac, and making returns to county seat of Newaygo Coun-

ty, 2 days' attendance, and 1500 miles travel,......... 78 00

Smith & Cowles, sundries for House of Representatives, under

Joint Resolution No 21, of 1853,............ .... 5 80

H. Gibbs, work done, ... $4 50
   "   "   by order of Senate, ... 5 50
Richard Elliot, candlesticks for House of Representatives, ... 6 00
Mrs. O. C. Wiswell, paste furnished House and Senate, ... 15 00
W. S. Whipple, stationery furnished, ... 757 30
A. Welch, services as watchman by order of House and Senate, 10 00
R. C. Madden, services as door-keeper of House of Representa-
   tives, 29 days at $3 per day, ... 87 00

April 20, 1853.
Geo. W. Peck, for binding Senate and House bills Sec. State, 10 00
   "   printing, binding, and pressing for Aud. Gen., 311 50
   "   and pressing for Land Office, ... 13 50
   "   "   Sec. State, ... 64 40
   "   ruling, &c., Land Office, ... 27 50
   "   binding, &c., State Treasurer, ... 28 50
   "   "   Sup't Pub. Inst'n, ... 511 50
   "   pressing, &c., Aud. Gen'l, ... 79 13
   "   ruling, &c.,   " 1040 00
   "   pressing, &c.,   " 87 50
   "   binding items for Sess. Laws, 1853, ... 157 50
   "   State Library, ... 13 50
   "   printing and composition Sess. Laws, 1853, .. 377 23
   "   annual reports Legislature, ... 306 36
   "   Manual 46 74
   "   Attorney Gen'ls Report, ... 13 08
   "   Tax Law for Aud. Gen'l, ... 58 84
   "   House and Senate Documents, 1853, 126 83
   "   "   "   bills, 1853, ... 939 36
   "   "   "   journals, 1853, ... 591 72
   "   pressing and folding Attorney Gen'ls Report, 6 28
   "   binding items Legislature, 1853, ... 627 58
   "   "   Tax Law Auditor General, ... 58 50
   "   "   manual, 1853, ... 175 00
   "   "   school laws, ... 500 00
   "   printing Saut Ste. Marie Canal Laws, ... 17 50
   "   "   "Yeas and Nays," for Leg. 1853, .. 25 00
   "   "   advertisement for office Sec'y State, .. 198 00

H. Doesburg, translating and printing Gov's message,........$106 00

April 21, 1853.

A. S. Wadsworth, for services selecting Saut Ste. Marie Canal
    lands,... 816 50
John Swegles, expenses to Detroit, State business,.......... 15 00
Levi Hunt, sundries furnished Capitol,.................... 8 07
C. W. Lewis, American almanac for Secretary State,........ 1 00
Mrs. Hamlin, washing,................................... 3 50
A. E. Hathon, services, Land Office,...................... 3 00
Otto Harmon,   "   as porter, &c.,................ 65 33
Edmonds & McReynolds, commission on sale of real estate,... 15 00
O. & A. Jordon, architectural drawing, &c.,............... 150 00
Israel Gillett, lumber, making boxes, &c.,................. 25 18
C. C. Hascall, services as trustee of Mich. Asylums,........ 33 00
D. V. Bell, Jr., " in Aud. Gen'ls Office,............... 3 30
A. V. Dearin, "   " 8 25
M. D. Cobb, express charges,............................ 1 88
S. W. Wright & Co., sundries furnished Senate, Jt. Resolution
    21 of 1853,... 4 86
C. Wakenhut, services,................................. 50
S. W. Wright & Co., bill of sundries for State offices,....... 28 72
Stanly Briggs,   "   " 2 50
S. W. Wright & Co., sundry articles furnished H. of Rep.,
    (under Joint Resolution No. 21 of 1853,)............ 22 40
Humphrey & Hibbard, transportation,.................... 3 00
B. F. Bush, stationery,................................. 49 94
John Swegles, deficiency in title of lands bought of State,.... 150 00
    "   board of porter,........................... 21 00
State Treasurer, payment of sundries,.................... 10 75
    "   coin scales, &c.,......................... 2 88
Humphrey & Hibbard, transportation,................... 30 41
E. H. Whitney, expenses to Detroit, for Treasurer,......... 2 50
Levi Hunt, articles furnished H. of Rep.,................. 4 00
E. G. Mixer & Co., trees for Capitol yard,................ 25 75
A. Ballard, tacks, &c.,................................. 1 00
Levi Hunt, bill of sundries for Capitol,................... 4 50
W. Whipple, sealing wax State Treasurer,................ 1 00

Francis Otteny, services as assistant porter,.............. $9 00

Henry Moots, making boxes, &c.,...................... 5 50

A. Miles, wood,.................................... 72 80

James Maguire, services as watchman,................. 51 00

Thompson & Godley, livery,......................... 10 00

Israel Gillett, services special messenger State Treasurer,.... 15 00

B. F. Bush, stationery for Land Office,............... 25 13

E. E. Beebe, supplies furnished Senate committee,......... 3 25

D. G. McClure,   "   "   "   44

A. Ballard,   -   - 1 58

S. Conant, services appraisement University lands,........... 5 00

D. Smart,   "   "   " 5 00

James A. Hicks,   "   ..   - 5 00

D. Kendall, constructing side walk, &c., in Detroit, on State
    property,.................................. 37 67

Stanly Briggs, building ditch, Lansing,.................. 91 80

Wm. S. Driggs, this amount paid on Primary School Land
    certificates, allowed under Joint Resolution No. 25, '53, 620 00

May 18, 1853.

H. L. & H. Baker, stock and labor, painting bridge at Lansing, 215 20

Geo. W. Peck, binding Sess. Laws of 1853, 4,500, @ 10c.,.... 450 00

J. H. Lobdell, amount allowed for surrendering lease of block
    249, Lansing,.................................. 8 00

J. Barnes & Co., printing, binding and stationery, by order of
    Sup. Court of Michigan,......................... 132 50

J. Barnes & Co., printing for Att'y Gen'l, notice to builders,.. 111 60

B. F. Bush, pens for Executive Office and for Reporter,..... 7 00

J. Van Rensselaer, services and sundry expenses ordered by Su-
    preme Court,.................................. 17 46

Samuel Chadwick, expenses in recruiting for Mexican war,... 256 76

May 20, 1853.

C. P. Bush, repairing roof of Capitol, as per contract,....... 40 00

July 7, 1853.

Whitney Jones, postage for Members of the Legislature, 1853,	$309	08
J. C. Frink, leasing swamp lands,...........................	10	50
Geo. B. Sherwood, services in office of Secretary of State,.....	133	00
Geo. D. Lathrop, services about Capitol,...................	5	50
Marshall Stage Company, transportation, Superintendent Public Instruction,..	4	00
Geo. T. Miller, services about Capitol grounds,...............	6	75
Henry Moots, making boxes for Secretary of State,..........	3	00
J. C. Bailey, expenses to Detroit, business for State,.........	10	50
Sheriff of Kalamazoo County, attendance on Supreme Court, &c.,..	10	50
E. Elliott, sundries for House of Representatives ordered by committee,..	3	12
State Treasurer, exchange on $18,290 remitted Phœnix Bank,	91	45
Edward McKibben & Co., furniture for public offices........	33	19
E. W. Cook, repairing lightning rods on tenant house,.......	2	00
State Land Office, 2 engrossing extension pen holders,.......	3	00
Henry Moots, repairs on State building,.................	22	00
John A. Bailey, seal press for Secretary of State,...........	35	00
B. F. Bush, transportation on paper for Auditor General,....	14	92
D. W. Buck, repairing furniture at Capitol,.................	4	51
B. F. Bush, bills of stationery for Land Office,.............	15	95
B. F. Bush, stationery for Treasurer's Office,..............	57	96
" bill of flat cap paper, and transportation,........	165	88
Whitney Jones, postage for State Offices, April 1 to May 5, 1853,..	40	19
Whitney Jones, postage for Auditor General, April 1 to May 5, 1853,..	78	60
Humphrey & Hibbard, transportation,....................	6	15
Stanley Briggs, sundries for Capitol,....................		88
B. C. Whittemore, postage and telegraph fees paid on official business,...	7	47
B. C. Whittemore, expenses to and from Detroit on official business,..	18	22
Van S. Murphy, postage for quarter ending June 30, 1853, Superintendent of Public Instruction,...................	4	50

Van S. Murphy, postage for quarter ending June 30, 1853,
State Treasurer,.. $10 13

Van S. Murphy, postage for quarter ending June 30, 1853,
Secretary of State,... 12 88

Van S. Murphy, postage for quarter ending June 30, 1853,
Commissioner of Land Office,............................. 10 30

Van S. Murphy, postage for quarter ending June 30, 1853,
Librarian,.. 4 67

Chapman & Pinckney, assignees of John Long, clearing streets
in Lansing,.. 35 81

Guile & Allison, repairing pen,............................. 50

Daily Times, publishing notice of sale of lands on River Rouge, 6 50

Humphrey & Hibbard, transportation,....................... 1 50

Ira Bennet, repairs on State House,......................... 1 00

Wm. Megiveron, work in Capitol yard,....................... 8 50

Levi Hunt, lumber and nails,............................... 12 51

B. F. Bush, stationery for House of Representatives ordered
by committee,... 23 81

B. F. Bush, stationery for Library,......................... 6 12

E. E. Beebe, sundries for Capitol,.......................... 2 56

State Treasurer, Thompson's Reporter,..................... 2 00

Wm. Megiveron, work done in and about Capitol yard,...... 136 25

J. A. Heimendinger,   "   " 23 75

      "   sawing wood for State Offices,........ 8 25

Stanley Briggs, nails and twine,........................... 1 78

R. Elliott, lath,... 1 00

J. M. Chase, gum arabic,................................... 38

Thompson & Godley, iron work for Capitol,................ 4 01

J. H. Lobdell, work done on block 79, Lansing,............ 6 25

Porter Kibbee, expenses to Detroit and Springwells, to attend
appraisal of University lands,............................ 15 00

Porter Kibbee, expenses to Detroit attending sale said lands, 18 50

      "   "   examining plan of public
offices,.. 7 00

O. & A. Jordon, balance of bill for plans and specifications
State offices,... 50 00

John Swegles, expenses to Flint, settling St. Amand defalcat'n, 15 00

Godley & Thompson, livery to Flint and back, Aud. General, $16 00
C. J. Fox, expenses to Flint, request Aud. Gen'l,........... 15 00
E. B. Pond, advertising forfeited school lands in Coldwater
   Sentinel...:..... 1 00
J. P. Baker, painting tenant house, Capitol,............... 90 00
Henry Moots, making 18 boxes,........................... 2 25
W. C. Ransom, express charges,........................... 1 50
H. L. & H. Baker, painting, glazing, &c., about Capitol,.... 32 00
M. T. Lyon, 6 boxes gutta percha pens,................... 15 00
A. W. Williams, thermometer for Senate, repairing clock, &c., 7 31
E. G. Mixer & Co., shrubbery for Capitol yard,............ 10 00
P. Kibbee, expenses to Detroit to attend meeting Board of Au-
   ditors, ... 15 00
J. P. Thompson, transportation,......................... 3 50
B. F. Bush, 62 reams crown paper for use of office Sup't of
   Public Instruction,.................................... 296 75
B. F. Bush, bill of stationery,........................... 188 70
     "   " 17 75
Guile & Allison, pens for Land Office,.................... 3 75
J. C. Bailey, expenses to Detroit and back, on business for the
   State,... 20 00
E. Elliott, pipe, setting up stove, &c.,.................... 2 88
   "   bill of pipe, wire, tin-ware, zinc, labor, &c.,....... 26 53

August 18, 1853.
Geo. W. Peck, printing for Sec. State,................... 6 50
     "   binding Session Laws 1853,............... 450 00
     "   printing and binding for Aud. General,...... 126 13
     "   pressing and folding Joint Doc's, Sen. and H.
          Journals of 1853,...................... 40 30
     "   printing title page and press work on same,... 7 53
     "   binding and ruling for Aud. General,....... 36 75
     "   pressing and ruling reports of school inspectors
          of townships for Sup't Pub. Instruction,.... 416 00
     "   binding Senate, House, and Joint Doc's 1853, 250 00
     "   "   reports and school laws of other States
          for Sup't Pub. Instruction,............... 18 50

Geo. W. Peck, printing, binding and ruling for Com'r of Land
            Office, ---------------------------- $39 41
      "   printing, ruling, and pressing for Aud. General, 200 25
              " and press-work Senate Journal, 1853, 199 06
               "   "   House   "   249 80
      "   pressing and folding reports of Sup't Pub. In-
            struction, and Doc's of Legislature 1853,... 156 00
      "   binding &c., for Land Office, swamp land maps, 17 70
      "   printing Report and accompanying Doc's Sup't
            Pub. Inst'n to Legislature of 1853, and press
            work on same,------------------------ 298 13

November 29, 1853.

D. P. Bushnell, correcting proof sheets, indexing and superin-
    tending publication of Journal and Documents of House
    of Representatives, session of 1853,-------------- 175 00

Bagg, Patton & McDonald, stationery furnished Geo. C. Gibbs,
    Reporter of the Supreme Court of Michigan,--------- 43 89

Wm. Hinman, sundry bills for State Offices,-------------- 131 17

Guile & Allison, pens for Secretary of State's Office,-------- 4 50

STATE OF MICHIGAN.

1853.

DOCUMENT No. 4.

ANNUAL REPORT of the Commissioner of the State Land Office.

STATE LAND OFFICE, }
Lansing, December 1, 1853. }

To His Excellency, ANDREW PARSONS, acting Governor of the State of Michigan:

Pursuant to the provisions of Act No. 154 of 1851, I have the honor to submit the following report, showing the business of this office for the fiscal year, ending November 30th, 1853:

SALES AND RECEIPTS

From December 1, 1852, to November 30, 1853, inclusive.

PRIMARY SCHOOL LANDS.

Sales.

Lots in Lansing,...................................			$28,874 00
December,	2,280.00	Acres,.......................	9,120 00
January,	1,853.81	"	7,415 24
February,	1,432.20	"	5,442 80
March,	3,542.	"	14,288 00
April,	2,529.79	"	10,119 16
May,	2,518.08	"	10,232 32

June,	3,885.08	Acres,	....	$15,540	32
July,	3,101.42	"	....	12,405	68
August,	4,498.30	"	....	18,405	20
September,	4,943.25	"	....	19,773	00
October,	7,402.36	"	....	29,609	44
Nov'mb'r,	10,863.70	"	....	43,895	00

48,850.04 Acres.   Total amount of sales of

School Lands, ...$225,160 16

Receipts.

| On account of principal, | .... | $107,417 | 20 |
| " interest and penalty, | .... | 43,664 | 65 |

Total receipts on account of School Lands, ... $151,081 85

UNIVERSITY LANDS.
Sales.

December,	394.90	acres,	....	$4,738	80
January,	399.78	"	....	4,797	30
February,	280.	"	....	3,360	00
March,	602.13	"	....	7,225	56
April,	1,057.22	"	....	17,615	65
May,	740.60	"	....	8,887	20
June,	758.17	"	....	9,619	80
July,	318.25	"	....	4,143	40
August,	860.80	"	....	11,153	55
September,	320.	"	....	3,950	00
October,	800.07	"	....	9,600	84
November,	829.17	"	....	9,950	04

7,361.49 acres.   Total amount of sales of Uni-
                                versity Lands, ... $95,042 20

Receipts.

| On account of principal, | .... | $34,984 | 44 |
| " interest and penalty, | .... | 11,287 | 97 |

Total receipts on account of University Lands, ... $46,272 41

NORMAL SCHOOL LANDS.

Sales.

2,227.98 acres,..$9,870 42

Receipts.

On account of principal,............................$3,909 79
    "   " interest and penalty,......................... 1,319 04

Total am't of receipts on acc't of Normal School Lands,..$5,228 83

ASYLUM LANDS.

Sales.

1,192.04 acres,..$4,768 16

Receipts.

On account of principal,............................$1,365 89
    "   " interest and penalty,..................... 345 02

Total am't of receipts on acc't of Asylum Lands,......$1,710 91

STATE BUILDING LANDS.

Sales.

111.12 acres,..$689 28
Lots in Lansing,... 1,207 00

Total am't of sales of State Building Lands,..........$2,096 28

Receipts.

Total am't of receipts on acc't of principal, interest, and
penalty,..$2,651 21

INTERNAL IMPROVEMENT LANDS.

Sales.

3,243.22 acres, at 10s ℔ acre,...........................$4,064 03

ASSET LANDS.

Sales.

Total amount of sales,..............................$720 00

SALT SPRING LANDS.

Receipts.

On acc't of principal and interest for lands sold prior to 1852, $1356 29

RECAPITULATION.

Total amount of Sales.

Of Primary School Lands,........................	$225,160	16
" University "	95,042	20
" Normal School "	9,870	42
" Asylum "	4,768	16
" State Building "	2,096	28
" Int. Improvement "	4,064	03
" Asset "	720	00
Total amount of sales,........................	$341,721	25

Receipts.

On account of Primary School Lands,............			$151,081 85
"	University	"	46,272 41
"	State Building	"	2,651 21
	Asylum	....	1,710 91
··	Normal School	"	5,228 83
"	Salt Spring	" ....-............ ...	1,356 29
	Asset	-	720 00
··	Int. Improvement	"	4,064 03
Total amount of receipts,.........................			$213,085 53

PRIMARY SCHOOL LANDS.

The sales of these lands for the last fiscal year, exceed the sales of 1852, about three hundred and seven per cent.

The sales in November amount to $44,218, and we may reasonably anticipate a corresponding increase for the coming year.

This large addition to the fund will be gratifying to the friends of Primary Schools throughout the State, and should stimulate them to urge the supremacy of Common Schools over all others, as upon them depend the very existence of higher seminaries, colleges, and universities.

Annexed, is given a list (marked "A") of the annual sales of these lands for 1843 to 1853, inclusive.

Statement (" B,") shows the comparative annual sales of lots in Lansing, since the location of the Capitol here.

UNIVERSITY LANDS.

The amount of sales of these lands during the year is 7,361.09 acres. This is 6,218.04 acres more than the sales of last year, and nearly equals the sales of the previous eight years inclusive, making the large addition to the fund of $95,042 20.

An effort was made in the late Legislature to reduce the price of these lands, particularly a fractional section in Spring Wells, Wayne county. Soon after the adjournment of that body, said section was subdivided and offered at public auction in Detroit, and sold at an average of $23 49 per acre.

The suit of ejectment, to which I referred in my last annual report, brought to recover possession of land lying near Toledo, claimed by the State, was decided last spring, adverse to the State. An appeal has been taken, which is now pending, and I have hopes that the title of the State will be finally maintained.

Statement (" C,") shows the comparative annual sales of these lands.

NORMAL SCHOOL LANDS.

It will be seen that the sales of these lands have more than doubled within the last year. Statement (" D,") exhibits the annual sales of these lands.

ASYLUM LANDS.

Statement marked (" E,") shows the comparative annual sales of these lands.

SWAMP LANDS.

We have received lists and diagrams of these lands for the Detroit and Kalamazoo land districts, amounting to 414,434.24 acres.

The public Press in some sections of the State have questioned the propriety of bringing these lands into market, and I deem it proper to explain my course in the premises. I have done simply what I conceive to be a duty required by the law providing for their sale.

The lists were received about four months since, and believing it a favorable time to offer them, I have given notice of the sale, a part of which are to be offered at Port Huron, and the balance at this Office.

Act No. 187, of 1851, provides that "the Commissioner of the State Land Office shall have the control and supervision of said lands, and of the sale thereof, and *shall as soon as the title vests in the State*, cause the same to be sold at public auction, at such times and in such quantities as he may think proper."

It will be seen by the provisions of the act above referred to, that the duty imposed upon the Commissioner is not discretionary, but *imperative.*

Sufficient information has been received at this office, to warrant the conclusion that this munificent donation amounts to over 5,000,000 of acres, a much larger area of acres than all prior grants by Congress to this State, and if prudently husbanded, will extinguish our State debt, after applying a reasonable amount for drainage, and leave a surplus to the cause of education.

What a State will Michigan be when free of debt—with a revenue beyond the wants of the State government, without taxation beyond the specific taxes provided by law.

All of which is respectfully submitted.

PORTER KIBBEE,
Commissioner.

[A.]

*Comparative Statement of the Sales of Primary School Lands,
deducting forfeitures.*

YEARS.	Acres.	Net amount sold after deducting all forfeited lands.	
Total amount of sales up to April 1st, 1843,	52,392.84	$369,264	39
Part year ending Nov. 30, 1843,..........	6,159.94	32,161	00
1 " " 1844,..........	7,454.66	38,860	60
1 " " 1845,..........	3,009.93	6,974	17
1 " " 1846,..........	6,879.63	35,169	70
1 including lots in Lansing, 1847,..........	18,350.32	91,501	63
1 " " 1848,..........	15,026.84	68,763	88
1 " " 1849,..........	8,946.66	38,509	74
1 " 1850,..........	10,978.79	47,111	26
1 1851,..........	19,189.95	83,449	89
1 1852,..........	12,602.59	52,709	89
1 1853,..........	48,850.04	225,160	16
Net sales of Primary School Lands,......	209,842.19	$1,089,636	31
Total amount of Primary School fund,.......... ...		$1,089,636	31

[B.]

Comparative Statement of Sales of Lots in Lansing.

1847,...	$18,233 00
1848,...	17,778 00
1849,...	5,631 00
1850,...	3,085 50
1851,...	6,828 00
1852,...	2,596 00
1853,...	30,081 00
Total amount of sales,........................	$84,232 50

[C.]

Comparative Statement of the Sales of University Lands, deducting forfeitures.

YEARS.	Acres.	Net amount sold after deducting all forfeited lands.
Total sales up to April 1, 1843,..........	$10,254 31	$123,209 90
Part year ending Nov. 30, 1843,.........	809 59	8,080 70
1 " " 1844,........	4,155 57	44,154 05
1 " " 1845,........	1,881 53	23,296 19
1846, ...	1,323 21	16,020 52
1847, ...	1,017 46	11,839 77
1848, ...	662 74	8,075 46
1849, ...	322 48	5,800 09
1850, ...	781 22	12,896 52
1851, ...	1,289 59	15,266 29
1852, ...	1,049 55	12,453 35
1853, ...	7,361 09	95,042 20
Net sales of University Lands,.........	$30,908 34	$376,135 04
Total amount of University fund,..............		$376,135 04

[D.]

Comparative Statement of Sales of Normal School Lands.

	Acres.	Am't sold for.
Total amount of sales to Nov. 30, 1850,.....	920.00	$8,600 00
One year ending Nov. 30, 1851,..........	3,215.98	13,524 19
" " 1852,..........	1,005.95	4,195 70
" 1853,...........	2,227.98	9,870 42
	7,369.91	$36,190 31
Less for forfeitures,..................... ...	200.00	720 00
Net sales of Normal School Lands,......	7,169.91	$35,470 31

[E.]

Comparative Statement of Sales of Asylum Lands.

	Acres.	Am't sold for.
Total amount of sales up to Nov. 30, 1850,....	460.00	$1,840 00
One year ending Nov. 30, 1851,.............	478.20	1,912 80
" " 1852,.............	680.00	2,720 00
" 1853,............1,192.04	4,768 16
	2,810.24	$11,240 96
Less for forfeiture in 1852,................	40.00	120 00
Net sales of Asylum Lands,.............	2,770.24	$11,120 96

STATE OF MICHIGAN.

1853.

DOCUMENT No. 5.

ANNUAL REPORT of the Inspectors of the State Prison for the year ending November 30th, A. D. 1853.

To His Excellency, ANDREW PARSONS, *acting Governor of the State of Michigan:*

The Inspectors of the State Prison transmit their Annual Report.

The following is an abstract of the monthly reports of the Agent to the Board of Inspectors during the year ending November 30th, A. D. 1853:

DECEMBER, 1852.

Cash on hand November 30th, 1852, as per annual report,.... $77 34

CASH RECEIVED THIS MONTH.

On account of State Treasury,................	$1000 00	
" convict labor,.................	96 58	
" convicts' deposits,.............	2 06	
" property sold, rent, &c.,.........	21 86	
" visitors....................	12 25	
		1,132 75
Total,....................................		$1,210 09

1

CASH EXPENDED THIS MONTH.

On account of building and repairs,	$484 89	
" clothing and bedding,	1 63	
" fuel,	42 18	
" oil and candles,	2 45	
" tobacco,	58 97	
" forage,	9 38	
" discharged convicts,	30 00	
" miscellaneous expenses,	1 00	
		630 48
Cash on hand,		579 61
Total,		$1,210 09

JANUARY, 1853.

Cash on hand, December 31st, brought forward, ... $579 61

CASH RECEIVED THIS MONTH.

On account of convict labor,	$825 75	
" property sold, rent, &c.,	3 00	
" visitors,	19 62	
		848 37
Total,		$1,427 98

CASH EXPENDED THIS MONTH.

On account of guards' wages,	$260 40	
" rations,	610 40	
" building and repairs,	108 99	
" clothing and bedding,	113 61	
" fuel,	153 07	
" hospital stores,	21 52	
" oil and candles,	75 51	
" library,	6 97	
" discharged convicts,	3 00	
" convicts' deposits,	3 00	
" stationery,	1 73	
" miscellaneous expenses,	26 58	
		1,384 78
Cash on hand,		43 20
Total,		$1,427 98

FEBRUARY, 1853.

Cash on hand January 31st, brought forward, ...$43 20

On account of State Treasury, ...$1,000 00
    "   convict labor, ...:   872 55
               visitors, ...   14 88
                                             ——— 1,887 43

   Total, ...$1,930 63

On account of officers' and keepers' salary, ...$326 17
    "   guards' wages, ... 317 63
               rations, ... 615 22
               building and repairs, ... 127 56
               clothing and bedding, ...   31 65
               fuel, ... 463 96
    "   forage, ...   21 91
               discharged convicts, ...   9 00
    "   convicts' deposits, ...   8 00
    "   miscellaneous expenses, ...   9 53
                                            ——— 1,930 63

MARCH, 1853.

CASH RECEIVED THIS MONTH.

On account of State Treasury,	$500	00
" convict labor,	2,771	61
property sold, rent, &c.,	35	00
visitors,	15	25
	$3,321	86

CASH EXPENDED THIS MONTH.

On account of officers' and keepers' salary,	$1,135	69
" guards' wages,	196	88
" rations,	551	21
building and repairs,	707	73
clothing and bedding,	270	85
fuel,	270	32
" hospital stores,	30	22
library,	1	66
" discharged convicts,	17	00
" miscellaneous expenses,	56	68
	$3,238	24
Cash on hand,	83	62
Total,	$3,321	86

APRIL, 1853.

Cash on hand March 31st, brought forward,..................$83 62

CASH RECEIVED THIS MONTH.

On account of State Treasury,...................$500 00
"   convict labor,....................1,040 31
"   convict deposits,................   75
"   property sold, rent, &c.,........... 82 63
"   visitors, ... 17 88
                                               ——————— 1,641 57

Total,...$1,725 19

CASH EXPENDED THIS MONTH.

On account of officers' and keepers' salary,.........$72 57
"   guards' wages,.....................278 77
"   rations,...........................605 95
"   building and repairs,..............544 54
"   clothing and bedding,.............. 56 22
"   fuel,.............................. 60 19
"   hospital stores,................... 4 50
"   discharged convicts,.............. 20 00
"   convicts' deposits,................   25
"   miscellaneous expenses,............ 14 52
                                               ——————— 1,657 51

Cash on hand,..................................... 67 68

Total,...$1,725 19

MAY, 1853.

Cash on hand April 30th, brought forward,................$67 68

CASH RECEIVED THIS MONTH.

On account of State Treasury,..................$1,000 00
    "   convict labor,........................ 649 38
    "   visitors,........................... 14 38
                              ——— 1,663 76

    Total,...$1,731 44

CASH EXPENDED THIS MONTH.

On account of officers' and keepers' salary,.........$63 77
    "   guards' wages,....................252 00
    "   rations,.........................610 40
    "   building and repairs,............184 34
    "   clothing and bedding,............169 61
    "   fuel, ... 57 40
    "   hospital stores,................. 1 90
    "   oil and candles,................151 13
    "   tobacco, ... 6 38
    "   forage, ... 6 60
    "   library,....................... 5 81
    "   discharged convicts,............ 21 50
    "   convicts' deposits,............. 2 00
    "   pursuing fugitives,.............116 00
    "   miscellaneous expenses,............ 3 07
                             ——— 1,651 91

Cash on hand,... 79 53

    Total,...$1,731 44

JUNE, 1853.

Cash on hand May 31st, brought forward,................ $79 52

CASH RECEIVED THIS MONTH.

On account of State Treasury,................	$1,000 00	
" convict labor,................	2,412 12	
property sold, rent, &c.,...........	28 50	
visitors,................	34 13	
		3,474 75
Total,................		$3,554 28

CASH EXPENDED THIS MONTH.

On account of officers' and keepers' salary,.....	$1,259 59	
" guards' wages,................	260 40	
– rations,................	617 90	
building and repairs,...........	373 64	
clothing and bedding,...........	452 35	
fuel,................	54 25	
hospital stores,................	119 97	
– oil and candles,................	47 32	
tobacco,................	25 41	
forage,................	21 00	
library,................	52 25	
– discharged convicts,................	15 00	
convicts' deposits,................	1 00	
stationery,................	7 81	
miscellaneous expenses,................	50 88	
		$3,358 27
Cash on hand,................		196 01
Total,................		$3,554 28

JULY, 1853.

Cash on hand June 30th, brought forward,..............$196 01

CASH RECEIVED THIS MONTH.

On account of State Treasury,..................$500 00	
" United States,.................. 123 12	
" convict labor,.................1,393 00	
" visitors, ... 58 48	
——————— 2,074 60	

    Total,....................................$2,270 61

CASH EXPENDED THIS MONTH.

On account of guards' wages,...................$297 78
" rations,......................... 594 59
" building and repairs,............ 602 72
" clothing and bedding,............ 322 20
" hospital stores,................. 63 53
" oil and candles,................. 90 76
" tobacco, ... 46 31
" forage, ... 6 60
" discharged convicts,............. 15 00
" agent's traveling expenses,...... 4 03
" miscellaneous expenses,.......... 59 00
                                             ——————— 2,102 52

Cash on hand,................................... 168 09

    Total,..................................$2,270 61

AUGUST, 1853.

Cash on hand July 31st, brought forward..............$168 09

CASH RECEIVED THIS MONTH.

On account of State Treasury,................$1,000 00
"   convict labor,.................... 645 02
"   visitors, ... 45 73
                     1,690 75

Total,..$1,858 84

CASH EXPENDED THIS MONTH.

On account of officers' and keepers' salary,..........$92 40
"   guards' wages,.....................260 40
"   rations,...........................615 96
"   building and repairs,..............388 38
"   clothing and bedding,............. 42 67
"   tobacco, ... 2 51
"   forage, ... 19 50
"   discharged convicts,.............. 8 00
"   convicts' deposits,............... 75
                     $1,430 57

Cash on hand,.. 428 27

Total,..$1,858 84

SEPTEMBER, 1853.

Cash on hand August 31st, brought forward,.............$428 27

CASH RECEIVED THIS MONTH.

On account of State Treasury,..................$1,000 00
     "   convict labor,.................. 1,775 73
     "   property sold, rent, &c.,..........   30 49
     "   visitors,.......................   71 71
                                 ————— 2,877 43

  Total,.....................................$3,305 70

CASH EXPENDED THIS MONTH.

On account of officers' and keepers' salary,.......$1,440 80
     "   guards' wages,.................   269 36
     "   rations, ...   607 72
     "   building and repairs,...........   104 35
     "   clothing and bedding,...........   106 42
     "   hospital stores,...............   95 63
     "   oil and candles,...............   43 79
     "   tobacco,......................   46 70
     "   library,.....................   9 00
     "   discharged convicts,............   26 50
     "   miscellaneous expenses,.........   37 65
                                 ————— 2,787 92

Cash on hand,..................................   517 78

  Total,.....................................$3,305 70

OCTOBER, 1853.

Cash on hand September 30th, brought forward,..........$517 78

CASH RECEIVED THIS MONTH.

On account of State Treasury,...............	$1,000 00	
"	convict labor,..................	732 76	
"	convicts' deposits,..............	3 10	
"	visitors, ...	108 57	
			1,844 43
Total,...................................			$2,362 21

CASH EXPENDED THIS MONTH.

On account of officers' and keepers' salary,........	$150 99	
"	guards' wages,................	266 64	
"	rations,......................	581 82	
"	building and repairs,..........	435 10	
"	clothing and bedding,.........	228 62	
"	hospital stores,..............	62	
"	forage, ...	19 38	
"	library,......................	11 62	
"	discharged convicts,..........	41 00	
"	convicts' deposits,............	3 38	
"	agent's traveling expenses,.....	34 50	
"	stationery, ...	10 59	
"	swine purchased,..............	119 00	
"	miscellaneous expenses,........	117 35	
			$2,020 61
Cash on hand,............................			341 60
Total,...................................			$2,362 21

NOVEMBER, 1853.

Cash on hand, October 31st, brought forward,............ ....$341 60

CASH RECEIVED THIS MONTH.

On account of State Treasury,.............. ....$1,000 00
"   convict labor,.................. ....1,888 19
"   convicts' deposits,..............   50
"   property sold, rent, &c.,...........   17 71
"   visitors,.....................   46 36
                                         ————— 2,952 76

Total,.................................... ....$3,294 36

CASH EXPENDED THIS MONTH.

On account of officers' and keepers' salary,........ $44 16
"   guards' wages,..................   533 36
"   rations, ...1,139 88
"   building and repairs,............   535 11
-        clothing and bedding,............   434 76
"   hospital stores,..................   10 45
"   oil and candles,................   93 18
            forage,......................   10 70
"   discharged convicts,..............   13 00
"   convicts' deposits,................   2 80
"   miscellaneous expenses,..........   31 23
                                     ————$2,848 63

Cash on hand,..   445 73

Total,.................................... ....$3,294 36

RECAPITULATION OF RECEIPTS AND EXPENDITURES FOR THE CURRENT YEAR.

Cash on hand as per last annual report,.................$77 34

CASH RECEIVED THIS YEAR.

On account of	State Treasury,..............	$9,500 00	
"	United States,...............	123 12	
	convict labor,................	15,102 50	
	convicts' deposits,...........	6 41	
	property sold, rent, &c.,.......	219 19	
	visitors, ...	459 24	
			25,410 46
Total,................................			$25,487 80

CASH EXPENDED THIS YEAR.

On account of	officers' and keepers' salary,....	$4,586 14	
"	guards' wages,..............	3,193 62	
	rations, ...	7,151 05	
"	building and repairs,..........	4,597 35	
	clothing and bedding,.........	2,230 59	
"	fuel,.......................	1,101 38	
"	hospital stores,...............	348 34	
"	oil and candles,..............	504 14	
"	tobacco,....................	186 25	
	forage,.....................	115 07	
	library, ...	87 31	
	discharged convicts,..........	219 00	
	convicts' deposits,............	21 18	
	pursuing fugitives, ...	116 00	
	agents' traveling expenses,.....	38 53	
	stationery,..................	20 13	
"	swine purchased,.............	119 00	
	miscellaneous expenses,........	406 99	
			25,042 07
Cash on hand,................................			445 73
Total,.....................................			$25,487 80

Table showing the number of convicts in Prison, and the manner in which they are employed on the 30th day of November, 1853.

Number of convicts in Prison, Nov. 30, 1852,.............. 209
   "   received during this year on sentence,............. 71
   "   retaken and returned,........................... 1
                                         —— 281
   "   discharged by expiration of sentence,............. 42
           "   pardon,........................... 24
           "   writ of habeas corpus,............ 1
   "   of deaths,.................................... 9
                                         —— 76

   "   remaining in Prison, Nov. 30, 1853.............. 205

These convicts are employed in the following manner:
By contractors, manufacturing farming tools,............. 91
    "   "   wagons and carriages,........ 53
    "   boots and shoes,............ 26
                                       —— 170
By the State, in building and repairing,.................. 6
    "   cook room,........................... 4
            tailors' shop,........................ 3
            preparing fuel,....................... 3
    "   wash room,.......................... 2
            prison hall,.......................... 2
   -         barbers' shop,........................ 1
   "   hospital,............................. 1
   ::   waiting about stables and agent's house,.... 1
   "   waiting about prison yard,............ 1
Unemployed, in solitary confinement,.................... 4
   "   on account of sickness and infirmity,........ 7
                                        —— 35

  Total,.. 205

There are white males,............................... 185
   "   "   females,.................................. 2
   "   colored males,............................. 18
                                        —— 205

*Table showing the average number of convicts, the average daily earn-
ings on contract, the total number of days labor performed for
contractors and for the State, also total amount earned on contract
during the year ending Nov. 30th, 1853.*

Average number of convicts,............................210
   "   daily earnings on contracts,.......................32¼c

		No. of days.	Earnings.
For contractors,	Pinney & Lamson,..............	28,377¼	$8,696 51
"	Davis, Austin & Co.............	13,887½	5,080 43
"	Walter Fish,...................	6,476	2,044 83
Total,..............................		48,740½	$15,821 27

		No. of days.
For the State,	in building and repairing,..........	1,372
"	wash room and cook room,........	2,110
"	prison hall and yard,..............	1,900
"	tailor's shop,.....................	983
"	barber's shop,.....................	312
"	hospital,..........................	313
Unemployed,	solitary confinement,..............	939
"	sick and infirm,...................	9,060½
Total number of working days spent in prison,		65,730

The following Tables show the Counties from which convicts have been sent during the year last past—the various crimes of which they were convicted, and the terms for which they were severally sentenced:

COUNTIES FROM WHICH SENT.

Wayne,	32
Hillsdale,	5
Washtenaw,	3
St. Joseph,	3
Van Buren,	3
Kalamazoo,	3
Jackson,	3
Lenawee,	3
Oakland,	2
St. Clair,	2
Monroe,	2
Kent,	2
Branch,	1
Cass,	1
Barry,	1
Ingham,	1
Berrien,	1
Calhoun,	1
Livingston,	1
Marquette,	1
Total,	71

Of what Crimes convicted.

Larceny,	38
Burglary and larceny,	4
Forgery,	4
Assault and battery with intent to kill,	3
Arson,	3
Burglary,	3

Receiving stolen goods knowing them to be such,.............. 3
Having in possession counterfeit bills with intent to pass the same,... 2
Rape,.. 2
Murder in 1st degree,... 2
Grand larceny,.. 2
Passing counterfeit money,... 1
Bigamy, ... 1
Perjury,... 1
Assault and robbery,.. 1
Larceny and breaking jail,.. 1
Breaking jail,.. 1
Assault with intent to commit rape,................................... 1
Assisting prisoner in attempt to escape,.............................. 1
Manslaughter,... 1
Obtaining property by false pretences,................................ 1
                                                                    ——
    Total,..71
                                                                    ══

TERMS OF SENTENCE.

For Life—solitary confinement, ... 2
 "   Fifteen years,... 2
 "   Twelve " 1
 "   Ten   " 2
 "   Seven   " 1
 "   Six   " 2
 "   Five   " 8
 "   Four   " 9
 "   Three   " 11
 "   Two years and six months,...................................... 1
 "   Two years,...12
 "   One year and six months,....................................... 4
 "   One year,..13
 "   Six months,.. 3
                                                                    ——
    Total,..71
                                                                    ══

The reports of the Agent, Physician and Chaplain, are hereto appended.

From the report of the Agent it appears that the actual earnings of the prison have been about $15,800; and the ordinary expenditures for maintenance and support, about $19,800; showing an excess of expenditures for ordinary purposes, above the actual income, of about $4,000. This excess cannot be much reduced during the existence of the present contracts. This will be a disappointment to many who, from former reports of the prison, have been induced to believe that the prison would soon become a self-sustaining institution. This cannot happen, in the exercise of the most rigid economy, until the existing contracts for the labor of the convicts expire; nor even then, unless there shall be more competition for convict labor than there has ever been heretofore.

At the last letting of contracts, great efforts were made to raise the price of labor, but to little purpose. The contract for the manufacture of wagons and carriages, had to be let at thirty-eight cents a day; that for boots and shoes at thirty-five cents, and that for farming tools at thirty-one cents. The average daily earnings of the one hundred and seventy convicts employed on contracts have been thirty-two and a half cents a day. At Auburn, in the State of New York, and Wethersfield, in the State of Connecticut, the same number of men would have earned on contracts, upwards of fifty cents a day. With labor at fifty cents a day, the prison would not only be a self-supporting institution, but prove a source of revenue to the State.

Under the direction of the Inspectors, the Agent has expended $3,776 21 in repairs and improvements. Of this amount, two hundred and seventy-six dollars were expended in the purchase of hose and fixtures; five hundred and thirty dollars in purchasing and dressing a sufficient quantity of stone for thirty-two new cells; nine hundred and thirteen dollars in the purchase of materials, and in grading and roofing a portion of the yard wall; four hundred and fifty-one dollars in re-laying with pine plank, the floor of the prison hall and lower tier of cells, and underlaying the same with charcoal; five hundred and forty-one dollars in the purchase and laying down of earthen and lead pipe for the purpose of conducting a supply of pure water into the prison yard; one hundred and thirty-two dollars in the purchase and putting up of stove pipe for warming the prison hall, and one hundred and seventy-five dollars in the purchase of cauldron kettles for washing and cooking.

All these repairs and improvements have been deemed necessary for the preservation of property, that, in its exposed condition, was rapidly going to decay and ruin, and for the improvement of the health and comfort of the convicts. The great number of days lost by sickness demonstrated the necessity of doing something to prevent, if possible, the recurrence of this evil. Such improvements as have been made, it is believed, will more than repay, during the coming year, every dollar that has been expended.

During the year the Inspectors have raised the salary of the physician from three hundred to four hundred dollars, and the pay of each of the guards from three hundred and seventy-five to four hundred dollars. They have also appointed an additional assistant keeper, at a salary of four hundred dollars, the same being allowed by law. The contract for rations, which was the lowest that could be obtained, has increased the expenditure under this head alone in the sum of two thousand five hundred and fifteen dollars and forty-one cents. This latter increase has been in part occasioned by an addition to the number of convicts, but mainly by the enhanced price of the rations. In the last annual report this increase was estimated at seventeen hundred dollars; it has been in fact over two thousand dollars.

The contract for supplying rations last year was taken at nine and a quarter cents for each day's ration. This was an increase over the preceding year of two cents four and a half mills. As no offer for the supply of rations, the coming year, was made at less than eleven cents and four mills for each day's ration, the Inspectors concluded that it would be a considerable saving to the State for the Agent to furnish the supply of provisions, and he has been accordingly so directed.

The Physician reports that there have been seven hundred and sixty-two applicants for admission to the hospital; of which five hundred and fifty were admitted, as follows, viz:

Typhoid fever, -- 27

Intermittent fever, -------------------------------------- 64

Diarrhœa, --113

Dysentery, --- 14

Ophthalmia, --- 16

Congestion of the brain,.. 2
    "   lungs,....................................... 2
Influenza, ... 17
Erysipilas,.. 5
Hemorrhage of the lungs,.................................... 2
Quinsy,.. 2
Inflammation of the lungs,.................................. 9
Asthma, ... 3
Rheumatism,.. 23
Colds, ... 63
Chronic affection of the lungs,............................. 9
Phthisis pulmonalis,.. 5
Chronic inflammation of the bowels,......................... 1
Hemorhoids, ... 11
Gonorrhea, ... 1
Syphilis, ... 4
Insanity, ... 3
Hernia, ... 7
Epilepsy,... 1
Chilblains,... 1
Sick for a day or two,......................................147

    Total,...552

During the year the convicts have suffered considerably from sick-ness. Nine have died—five of typhoid fever; one of chronic inflam-mation of the bowels; two of phthisis pulmonalis, and one of conges-tion of the brain. The typhoid fever made its appearance about the middle of April, and continued until the close of August. The cases of intermittent fever, diarrhœa, rheumatism, and congestion of the lungs, liver and bowels have been very much diminished. This year there have been two hundred and two of this class of cases; last year there were three hundred and sixty-seven. A further diminution of the more pre-valent diseases is anticipated, from the improvements which have been made in the prison yard, hall, and work shops.

    The Chaplain, who held the office till the first of September, reports that he visited the prisoners at their cells and in their workshops as often as his other avocations would admit. There have been religious services every Sabbath in the chapel. A Sunday School has been attended by some thirty of the boys and young men. Want of teachers has prevented the giving of Sunday School instruction to a greater number. Aside from these exercises, it has been the business of the chaplain to instruct several of the convicts in the principles of reading, writing and arithmetic. Instruction beyond these principles has not been entered upon, but it is in contemplation to enter upon it as soon as circumstances will permit. The young men and boys who are sent to the prison ought to receive daily instruction in the elementary branches of an English education, in order that when they go forth again into society they may be the better instructed and prepared to earn an honest livelihood.

The Legislature, at their last session, made it the duty of the Inspectors to prescribe the plan for a building in which to imprison all convicts sentenced to solitary confinement at hard labor for life, and appropriated the sum of $5,000 towards the erection of such building. No plan has been prescribed and nothing has been done under the appropriation. The sum appropriated was not sufficient for the erection of such a building, and as the legislature would not be again regularly in session until the year 1855, it has not been deemed expedient to commence the erection until the coming season.

The death penalty for murder was abolished by the revised statutes of 1846, and solitary confinement, at hard labor, in the State Prison for life, substituted. The latter provision took effect on the second day of March, 1847. Since that time—a period of almost seven years—there have been eleven persons sentenced to solitary confinement for life. In every instance where a murder has been committed, the jury have been prompt in the discharge of their duties, and in no case, it is believed, has there been a disagreement in the verdict.

The convicts sentenced to solitary confinement from the first day of March, 1847, to the second of April, 1849, were kept shut up in the cells of the Prison. It was soon ascertained that such confinement was rapidly wasting away the lives of the occupants. On a representation of the fact, the Legislature, by the act of the second of April, authorized the release of the convicts sentenced to solitary confinement, and their employment as other convicts, whenever, and for such times as the Inspectors might by resolution direct. The Inspectors have accordingly from time to time by resolution directed a release, and the employment as prescribed by statute. The convicts thus released, with a solitary exception, have ever conducted themselves with propriety, and evinced a willing disposition to conform to all the rules and regulations of the Prison.

The Inspectors cannot conclude this report without expressing their approbation of the manner in which the Agent, as well as the other officers, have discharged their respective duties. The situation of each is one of high responsibility, and yet this has been met in a spirit worthy of commendation.

ISAAC E. CRARY,
J. B. PIERCE,
R. R. THOMPSON.

JACKSON, December, A. D. 1853.

Agent's Report.

MICHIGAN STATE PRISON OFFICE, }
Jackson, December 1st, 1853. }

To the Board of Inspectors:

GENTLEMEN—In conformity to the requirements of the statute, I respectfully submit the following report of the transactions of this Prison during the fiscal year ending November 30th, 1853:

The whole number of convicts in Prison on the date of the last annual report, was.. 209

During the year ending with the date hereof, there has been received on sentence,.. 71

And retaken,.. 1
                                                                        ——
Total,... 281

During the same period there have been discharged—

By expiration of sentence,.................................... 42

By pardon,... 24

By writ of habeas corpus,..................................... 1

And there have died,.. 9
                                                             ——
                                                                        76

Leaving in prison at the present time,........................ 205

These convicts are now being employed in the following manner, to-wit:

By Pinney & Lamson, manufacturing farming tools,.........91

By Davis, Austin & Co., manufacturing wagons and carriages,..53

By Walter Fish, manufacturing boots and shoes,..............26
                                                             ——
Total number on contract,.. 170

By the State—

In building and repairing,.. 6

In cook room,... 4
In tailor shop,.. 3
In preparing fuel,....................................... 3
In wash room,... 2
In prison hall,.. 2
In barbers' shop,.. 1
In hospital,... 1
In waiting about stable and agent's house,............... 1
In waiting about prison yard,............................ 1

    Total number employed by the State,......................24
There are confined in solitary cells,..................... 4
And there are unemployed by reason of sickness and infirmity, 7
                           11

    Total,..205

The daily average number of convicts during the year, has been..210
The daily average number of last year, was.................186$\frac{1}{2}$

Average daily increase,................................. 23$\frac{1}{2}$

The total number of working days spent in prison during the same
    time, is..65,730
Of this number there have been employed on contract, at an
    average daily price of about 32$\frac{1}{2}$ c.,........................48,740$\frac{1}{2}$

Leaving to be accounted for,............................16,989$\frac{1}{2}$

    There has been employed in the service of the State—
In building and repairing,.............................1,872
In wash room and cook room,...........................2,110
In prison hall and yard,...............................1,900
In tailors' shop,....................................... 983
In waiting,.. 626
In barber's shop,...................................... 312
In hospital,... 313

    Total number employed on State work,................ 7,616
There has been spent in solitary confinement,......... 939

And lost, by reason of sickness and other causes,......8,434½
                                                      ——— 9,373½

Total,..16,989½

On the first day of May last, when I assumed the duties of Agent of this Prison, five months of the fiscal year had elapsed. Up to that time as appears from the books in the clerk's office, the total cash receipts of my predecessor, including $77 73, balance on hand at the date of the last annual report, amounted to the sum of....$8,909 32 and the total disbursements to the same period were...... 8,841 64

leaving a cash balance on hand of................... **$67 68**

There were also outstanding demands against the Prison, for building materials, and ordinary supplies, furnished to that date, amounting to the sum of................................... $2,011 99
If to this sum be added the amount disbursed by my predecessor, as above stated,............................ 8,841 64

it will appear that the total expenditures on account of the Prison at that time, was..............................$10,853 63

Since the above mentioned date there has been received into the Prison treasury, including $67 68 cash on hand, the sum of $16,578 48
Which together with the amount previously received, 8,909 32

Makes the total cash receipts for the year amount to the sum of $25,487 80

The sources from which this sum has been realized, are as follows, to wit:

Cash on hand as per last annual report,................	$77 73
From State Treasury for Inspector's certificates,.........	9,500 00
" United States for support of convicts,...........	123 12
" contractors for convict labor,.................	15,102 50
" sundry persons for property sold, rent, &c.,........	219 19
" visitors for admission fees,...................	459 24
" convicts for money deposited,.................	6 41
Total,..	$25,487 80

During the same period there has been paid out in liquidation of outstanding demands, and for other purposes, the sum of..$16,201 01

To which, add the amount paid by my predecessor,....... 8,841 06

Gives for the total disbursements during the year, the sum of $25,042 07

Leaving a cash balance on hand, of.................... $445 73

This sum has been expended for the following purposes, to-wit:

On account of officers' and keepers' salary,................$4,586 14

"   guards' wages,.......................... 3,193 62

"   rations, ... 7,151 05

"   building and repairs,.................... 4,597 35

"   clothing and bedding,.................... 2,230 59

"   fuel,.................................... 1,101 38

"   hospital stores,......................... 348 34

"   oil and candles,......................... 504 14

"   tobacco,................................. 186 25

"   forage,.................................. 115 07

"   library, ... 87 31

"   discharged convicts,..................... 219 00

"   convicts' deposits,...................... 21 18

"   pursuing fugitives,...................... 116 00

"   stationery,.............................. 20 13

"   swine purchased,......................... 119 00

"   agent's traveling expenses,.............. 38 53

"   miscellaneous expenses,.................. 406 99

Total,...................................$25,042 07

The whole amount of outstanding demands against the prison, at the close of the year is,..............................$2,174 16

To meet this indebtedness there is due the prison—

From contractors for convict labor,............$1,330 43

From United States for support of convicts,..... 175 53

From all other sources,......................... 23 75

And cash on hand,............................... 445 73

Total,.....................................1,975 44

Leaving a balance against the prison of,.................$198 72

If therefore, to the outstanding demands,.................$2.174 16

Be added the total amount of disbursements,..............25,042 07

—The expenditure for all purposes during the year would appear to be,..$27,216 23

There has, however, been disbursed this year on account of building and repairs, the sum of,.............$1,069 91 that was expended for that purpose, during the previous year.   In like manner there has been paid this year for ordinary support, the sum of,....   78 52

Making the total disbursements this year on account of the previous year's business, amount to the sum of,... 1,148 43

Which if deducted from the sum above stated, shows the actual expenditures for the current year to be...........$26,067 80

The total cash disbursements this year, on account of building and repairs, as has already been stated, amount to the sum of..$4,595 35

The outstanding demands that should be carried to this account are,.. 248 77

Making the sum of,.....................................$4,846 12

From which deduct the amount which should have been paid and reported last year, as above stated,.............. 1,069 91

And it will be seen that the total expenditures on account of building and repairs, during the current year, has been..$3,776 21

This sum has been disbursed in the following manner, and for the following purposes, to-wit:

For the purchase of about six hundred feet of vulcanized India rubber hose, and the necessary fixtures, to be worked in connection with a large sized force pump, for the purpose of protecting the Prison buildings from destruction by fire,.......................$276 69

For the purchase of, and dressing a sufficient quantity of stone for thirty-two additional new cells, together with thirty-two cast iron arms for gallery walk,.................... 530 68

For the purchase of material, grading, and roofing about eleven hundred feet of the yard wall, and building three guard houses on the same,... 913 50

For relaying the floor in the Prison hall, and lower tier of cells, with two inch pine plank, and underlaying the same with charcoal about six inches in depth, and the purchase of materials therefor,.. 451 40

For the purchase of, and laying down one hundred rods of earthen pipe, and about the same length of lead pipe, for the purpose of conducting a supply of pure water into the Prison yard,.. 541 95

For the purchase of, and putting up about five hundred feet of eleven inch stove pipe for warming Prison hall,......... 132 13.

For the purchase of six large sized cauldron stove kettles, to be used for washing, and culinary purposes,.... .... 175 51

For electrical conductors on Prison buildings,........... 80 00

For building two sheds in Prison yard for storing stone and wood,... 68 00

For the purchase of lumber for fence,................... 65 45

And for other minor repairs about the Prison, all of which were necessary to preserve the property of the State from decay, ... 540 91

    Total,...$3,776 21

It therefore appears, from the foregoing statement, that the total amount expended during the year just closed, for the ordinary support of the Prison, including salaries of officers, keepers, and guards, is.. $21,221 68

And that the total income from the Prison during the same period, is... 17,516 98

Showing an excess of expenses for support over income from Prison, of... $3,704 70

In view of the encouragements held out to the Inspectors, as well as the public, in the last annual report of my predecessor, that it might be confidently expected that this Prison would very soon, if not during the

year just closed, become a self-supporting institution, and cease to require
any further aid from the public treasury, it would have been extremely
gratifying, had facts warranted a more favorable report of its financial
transactions since that date.   It is difficult, however, to see how, under
the circumstances, a different result could have been reached.

The expenditures for building and repairs have been made under the
direction of your Board, and certainly do not exceed the amount actually
required.   Indeed, it is believed, that a just regard for the public interest, and the exercise of an enlightened economy, would have warranted
a much larger outlay for that purpose.   The amount expended on
account of salaries, as well as the appropriation for the library, is established by law, and is entirely beyond the control of the Agent, either
to increase or diminish.   And it is not difficult to show that a variety
of causes have been operating, during the past year, to greatly augment
the expenditures for ordinary supplies over former years, equally beyond the control of the Prison authorities.   The most prominent of
these causes is to be found in the enhanced market value of these
supplies.

For the single article of rations, there has been paid, during the current year, over and above what they would have cost at last year's
prices, the sum of.. $1,888 80
And the same cause has effected equally, and in like manner, the
expenditure for all articles required for Prison consumption.   In addition to this, it was found necessary in the early part of the year to create
a new keepership, at a salary of $400 per annum, and about the same
time the salary of the physician was increased from $300 to $400, and
the wages of the guards raised from $375 to $400 per annum, all of
which had a direct tendency to increase expenses for the ordinary
supplies.

Now, if it be borne in mind that there is no corresponding increase
in the amount received for convict labor, but, that the price of that
labor is established beyond the possibility of change during the existence
of present contracts, at the low rate of about $32\frac{1}{2}$ cents per day, it is at
once evident what effect this state of things must have upon the finances of the Prison.

Most of the reports heretofore emenating from this office, that have
come under my observation, have seemed to proceed upon the princi-

ple, that to make the Prison pay expenses, and if possible, yield an income to the State, was the great and paramount desideratum to be secured. That the exercise of a rigid economy in all the various departments, is a duty incumbent upon the officers in charge, must be admitted; yet it is believed that there are considerations to be taken into the account, in the administration of Prison affairs, of vastly more importance to the public at large, than the mere question of dollars and cents. The great and leading design of the people, in the establishment of such an institution, was not to secure an income therefrom, but protection to their lives and property, and reformation, as far as may be, in the character of its inmates. The addition of hard labor to the sentence of confinement in the State Prison, as a penalty for the commission of crime, was adopted as much, if not more, for the benefit of the convict in the preservation of his health, both mentally and physically, as to secure the price of his services. So far, however, as such labor can be made to produce a revenue, without defeating the main object for which it was designed, it is well. Most of our convicts, after serving out a short sentence, are discharged, to mingle again with the citizens and youth of the land. If, therefore, the main object in the establishment of prison disciple be lost sight of in an undue anxiety to secure an income therefrom, there is great danger that they will be sent abroad, unreformed, to renew their depredations upon, and corrupt the morals of society; so that however much may have been gained in a pecuniary point of view, the public will be the loser in the end.

Much sickness has prevailed among the convicts during the past season. In addition to the ordinary diseases of the country, an epidemic broke out in the latter part of the Spring, which proved fatal to several of the convicts, and bid fair at one time, to become general throughout the prison. Fortunately, however, by the prompt adoption of sanatory measures, and the vigilant care and attention of the acting physician, the disease was soon arrested. Everything has been done that could be, to remove all causes of sickness from the prison buildings and yard, and restore the health of the convicts, which, it gives me great pleasure to say, is at the present time unusually good. But few cases of sickness now exist, and those mostly of a chronic character of long standing, and such as will be found to prevail to a greater or less extent in all institutions of this kind. It is to be hoped as well on account of the suffering of the convicts, as the great loss of income from their inability to labor, that they will in future be relieved from any such amount of sickness as has prevailed during the year just closed.

A general feeling of contentment and cheerfulness seems to prevail among the convicts, and in most cases a disposition is manifested to obey the rules of discipline and perform their allotted task without complaint.

The subordinate officers now in charge, are vigilant and attentive to their duties, and it is believed that the discipline of the prison is being well administered.

Believing, gentlemen, that the foregoing embraces all the material facts which the law makes it my duty to report to your Board, you will permit me in conclusion, to tender my sincere thanks for the aid and assistance that I have received at your hands, during our official intercourse.

PETER DOX, *Agent*.

Physician's Report.

To the Inspectors of the State Prison:

In conformity with usage, I submit the subjoined report of the Hospital Department:

The amount of sickness and number of deaths among the convicts during the year have been unusually large. The whole number who have applied for admission to the hospital is seven hundred and sixty-two, of whom five hundred and fifty-seven were admitted. Of these, some have been under treatment many days, others for less periods. In addition to the endemical diseases of the country, the typhoid fever, in an epidemic form, made its appearance about the middle of April, and continued until near the close of August. The whole number of deaths has been nine; of which five were of typhoid fever, and the remainder of the following diseases: one of chronic inflammation of the bowels; two of phthisis pulmonalis, and one of congestion of the brain.

The cases which have been prescribed for, are as follows: typhoid fever, 27; intermittent fever, 64; diarrhœa, 113; dysenterry, 14; ophthalmia, 16; congestion of the brain, 2; congestion of the lungs, 2; influenza, 17; erysipelas, 5; hemorrhage of lungs, 2; quinsy, 2; inflammation of lungs, 9; asthma, 3; rheumatism, 23; colds, 63; chronic affection of lungs, 9; phthisis pulmonalis, 5; chronic inflammation of bowels, 1; hemorrhoids, 11; gonorrhea, 1; syphilis, 4; insanity, 3; hernia, 7; epilepsy, 1; chilblains, 1; sick for a day or two. 147.

G. W. GORHAM,
Physician.

Chaplain's Report.

To the Inspectors of the Michigan State Prison:

GENTLEMEN :—Having officiated as Chaplain to the State Prison for six months of the past year, it becomes my duty to report to you the religious and moral condition of the prisoners during that time, and the state of the Prison Library, the charge of which is committed to the Chaplain.

I was re-appointed to the office of Chaplain the 1st of March last, and accepted the appointment with the understanding that the arrangement was only temporary, that I was to officiate only until a suitable person could be obtained to devote his whole time to the duties of the office; my engagements as rector of a parish, being such as to render a proper discharge of the duties of Chaplain impossible.

Having been connected with the prison for the space of two and a half years, I can truly say that I have never been more interested in any field of labor, and know of none that will more abundantly repay a devoted and enlightened culture. Such is my opinion of the good to be realized to these convicts by a faithful discharge of the duties of Chaplain, and such the interest which their wants, their ignorance of the first principles of christian knowledge and their desire for instruction, have awakened within my mind, that had the remuneration of the office been adequate to the support of my family, I should have been disposed to devote myself exclusively to the great work of instruction and reform so much needed in this institution.

Hardly had I entered on the duties of my office, before an alarming and fatal sickness broke out among the prisoners, which within the space of two months carried eight of them to their graves, besides one valuable keeper. During the whole of this time I visited the prison daily, to instruct and console the sick, and to prepare them to meet death in the spirit of christianity—with resignation and without alarm. To one prisoner, whose recovery was regarded as nearly hopeless, and who manifested a great desire for that rite, I administered the sacra-

ment of baptism. He however, recovered, and through the clemency
of the Executive, has been pardoned and restored to his family.

It is with pleasure, as well as a matter of duty, that I bear testimony
to the excellent care bestowed upon the sick by the prison authorities;
the attention paid to their wants, and the relief of their sufferings, the
procurement of whatever tended to promote their comfort and aid their
recovery; and the prompt and efficient measures taken to cleanse the
prison from all impurities, and to remove certain local causes, which in
the judgment of some contributed to the production of the disease, or
to render its nature more virulent and less likely to yield to proper
medical treatment. While alluding to this subject, it may not be considered as impertinent to the objects of this report, if I briefly refer to
certain improvements in the Prison designed to promote the comfort
of the prisoners as well as the preservation of their health. I allude
particularly to the increased facilities for warming the prison; while at
the same time they exclude that dense cloud of smoke which for years
has filled the prison to the discomfort and annoyance of all connected
with it. Among men strangled by smoke and shivering with cold,
it would seem to be a difficult task to maintain a rigid and wholesome
discipline. I have referred to this subject only because of the happy
influence which all such improvements have upon the prisoners, in pro-
ducing among them cheerfulness and contentment, as well as a disposition to perform with a good will the tasks assigned them.

The prisoners have been visited as often as convenient, both in the
workshops, and at their cells, and I have endeavored to render effectual
my instructions, by impressing upon them in private, what was delivered
to them in the public exercises of the chapel. The religious services
on Sunday have been as usual; a Sunday school in the morning, which,
owing to the want of suitable teachers, has been necessarily limited to
twenty-five or thirty convicts, mostly boys and young men, and preach-
ing in the chapel in the afternoon. To all these services the prisoners
listen with close attention, and they are somewhat celebrated for the
strict propriety with which they conduct themselves during the perform-
ance of our public services. Upon not a few I have reason to believe
that these services have had a most happy influence; upon all, I have no
doubt, they have had a restraining influence, tending to facilitate the
maintenance of a sound discipline. If the influence, which a faithful

and prudent Chaplain brings to bear upon the minds of the prisoners were withdrawn, the authorities of the Prison would find it a much more difficult task to keep them within the limits of the prescribed regulations. Religious truths, with the sanctions attending them, forcibly presented, and constantly kept before the minds of even bad men, have a most salutary and restraining tendency.

The annual appropriation for the library has been expended in the purchase of suitable books for the prisoners. These books were submitted to the clerk of the Prison, whom you have made the adviser of the Chaplain in their purchase, and received his approval. Such are the wear and tear of books in this Institution, that the appropriation of one hundred dollars but barely keeps up the library. About as many books are annually destroyed as are purchased. It has been heretofore the policy of the Chaplain to obtain as *many* books as possible with the means placed in his hands, for the reason, that the prisoners, like most men, are fond of *new* things, though, in the judgment of some, the *old* are far better. In order to gratify this desire for new books, such as are lightly and cheaply bound have usually been purchased. I would, however, suggest, that, for the future, no books but such as are well and strongly bound be added to the Prison library. Although the cost of such would be greater, and, consequently, a smaller number annually added to the library, still it would be economy, and the best means of *increasing* the library.

Permit me, in conclusion, to suggest, that, whereas there are in this State no Houses of Correction for juvenile offenders, where they are subjected to all needful restraints, their morals properly cared for, and themselves instructed in the elements of a sound education, and whereas, until such Houses shall be established, a large and increasing class of such offenders must be confined within the State Penitentiary; whether some means cannot be devised by which these boys shall receive daily instruction in the elementary branches of an English education? Such provision is made in all of our Eastern Prisons, and in the majority of those located in the West. And when we take into consideration the fact, that these boys are confined here only for a limited time, and are soon to go forth again into society, from which their offences have for a season excluded them, is it not the interest of the State, and the dictate of a sound policy, that they should go forth better instructed and better prepared to earn an honest livelihood? Would not *one hour* of each day devoted to such a purpose, be productive of more permanent, real benefit to the State, than all the avails of their material labor for that time? Regarding the subject of the very first importance, I have thrown out the suggestion, believing that it will receive your prompt and candid attention.

In the discharge of my official duties, the Agent of the Prison has kindly rendered me every needed facility.

On the first of September, the Rev. Mr. Clement, of the Methodist Episcopal Church, having, upon my resignation, been appointed to succeed me in the chaplaincy, entered on his duties. I have no doubt he will devote himself faithfully to the important duties committed to his hands.

Respectfully yours,
DAN'L T. GRINNELL.

STATE OF MICHIGAN.

1853.

DOCUMENT No. 6.

ANNUAL REPORT of the Attorney General.

ATTORNEY GENERAL'S OFFICE,
Lansing, January 1, 1854.

To His Excellency, ANDREW PARSONS, Governor of Michigan:

SIR—In obedience to the requirements of law, I submit herewith my report of the business of this office for the year one thousand eight hundred and fifty-three.

The case of the People, at the relation of one of my predecessors against the President, Directors and Company of the Macomb County Bank, was argued and submitted at the last January term. In this case, it will be seen by reference to my last annual report, that an appeal was taken to the Supreme Court, from the decree of the Judge of the Circuit Court of Wayne county, sitting as Chancellor. The decree of the latter Court, dismissing the bill filed in the case, was sustained, affirming in effect the validity of the charter.

In the month of February last, I filed an Information in the nature of a quo warranto, at the relation of D. Darwin Hughes, Esq., against Charles S. May, to enquire by what authority he assumed to exercise the office of Prosecuting Attorney of Calhoun. At the general election of the preceding November, the respondent received a majority of the votes for that office, but it was claimed that he was ineligible, not being, at the time of his election, an attorney at law. The case was

1

argued and submitted at the July term, but the court being equally divided in opinion, a re-argument was ordered.

In the case of the people against Henry I. Higgins, on an Information to enquire by what warrant he exercised the office of Judge of Probate of Genesee county, judgment of ouster was pronounced at the Kalamazoo term of the Supreme Court, and the relator, Warren Lake, Esq., declared to be entitled to the office. The proceeding was based upon various errors in the action of the board of canvassers, in the allowance and rejection of votes.

Prior to the last July term, I filed in the Supreme Court, Information against the Michigan Southern and the Erie & Kalamazoo Railroad Companies. The proceedings were commenced at the relation of Ira N. Grosvenor, acting as the agent and attorney of numerous citizens of Monroe, who felt themselves aggrieved, in consequence of the diversion of trade and travel from the city of Monroe to Toledo, by the way of the Erie & Kalamazoo Railroad. It was averred in the complaint of the relator, that the connection of the two roads at Adrian was unauthorized; that it changed practically the eastern terminus of the Michigan Southern Railroad; that the Michigan Southern Railroad Company had violated it in leasing for its use the road from Adrian to Toledo; and that the Erie & Kalamazoo Railroad Company had, by the terms of the lease, virtually surrendered its franchises.

The following cases, brought before the Supreme Court by writs of error, were argued and submitted at the January term, viz: Schweitzer, vs. the people; Mills, vs. the people; and Showerman, vs. the people. In the two first named cases, the verdicts were set aside and new trials granted.

The schedule herewith annexed, marked "A," contains the facts of the reports of the several Prosecuting Attorneys of this State, so far as they have been received at this office.

All which is respectfully submitted.

WILLIAM HALE,
Attorney General.

ABSTRACTS

OF

THE REPORTS

OF

PROSECUTING ATTORNEYS.

Schedule "A"

ABSTRACTS OF REPORTS OF PROSECUTING ATTORNEYS.

*Allegan County—*HENRY C. STOUGHTON, ESQ., *Prosecuting Attorney.*

CLASS I.—CASES PROSECUTED BY INDICTMENT.

Names of persons prosecuted.	Offence charged.	Month and year of indictment.	When disposed of.	How disposed of, punishment, if any, or present condition of the case.	Remarks
Nelson Knight,	Rape.	Oct., 1853.		In jail, awaiting trial.	
William G. Butler,	False pretences.	do		Still pending.	

CLASS II.—CASES PROSECUTED OTHERWISE THAN BY INDICTMENT.

Names of persons prosecuted.	Offence charged.	Mode of prosecution.	In what court, whether before a justice or other magistrate.	When commenced.	When disposed of.	How disposed of, punishment, if any, or present condition of the case.	Remarks
Martha Chambers,	Obstructing highway.	Action of debt.	Justice of the Peace.	Nov. 1.		Still pending.	
Osmond Smith,	Treasurer's bond.	Debt.	Circuit Court.			Case withdrawn.	

*Barry County—*J. A. HOLBROOK, ESQ., *Prosecuting Attorney.*

CLASS I.—CASES PROSECUTED BY INDICTMENT.

Names of persons prosecuted.	Offence charged.	Month and year of indictment.	When disposed of.	How disposed of, punishment, if any, or present condition of the case.	Remarks.
John B. Allen,	Larceny.	May, 1853.	Nov. 1853.	Acquitted.	
William H. Hayford,	Perjury.	do		Not disposed of.	
Amos and Nathaniel Barry,	Nuisance.	do		do	
Corydon Y Deal,	Larceny.	do	May, 1853.	Pled guilty.	Sentenced State prison 3 years.
Benjamin M Burr,	Adultery.	do		Not disposed of.	

CLASS II.—CASES PROSECUTED OTHERWISE THAN BY INDICTMENT.

Names of persons prosecuted.	Offence charged.	Mode of prosecution.	In what court, whether before a justice or other magistrate.	When commenced.	When disposed of.	How disposed of, punishment, if any, or present condition of the case.
John Cole,	Assault and battery,	Complaint	Justice of the Peace.	April, 1853.	April, 1853.	Convicted and fined
John Dawson,	do	"	"	June, 1853.	June, 1853.	
William Salmson,	Larceny.	"	"			A bsconded
Charles F Sedgwick,	Assault and battery,	"	"			Convicted and fined
John L. McLellan,	Selling liquor to Indians			June, 1853.	June, 1853.	Acquitted

Berrien County—JAMES BROWN, Esq., Prosecuting Attorney.

CLASS I.—CASES PROSECUTED BY INDICTMENT.

Names of persons prosecuted.	Offence charged.	Month and year of indictment.	When disposed of.	How disposed of, punishment, if any, or present condition of the case.	Remarks.
Charles E. Smith,	Having counterfeit money in possession, with intent to pass the same.	March, 1853	Sept., 1853.	Nolle prosequi entered.	
Charles Schirk,	Larceny.				
Samuel Cardinsky,	Rape.	June, 1853	June, 1853	Not disposed of. Convicted	Sentenced to State prison 10 years
Richard Ene.	Larceny.				

CLASS II.—CASES PROSECUTED OTHERWISE THAN BY INDICTMENT.

Names of persons prosecuted.	Offence charged.	Mode of prosecution.	In what court, whether before a justice or other magistrate.	When commenced.	When disposed of.	How disposed of.
Samuel Maddox,	Threats.	Complaint	Justice of the Peace.	Feb., 1853	February, 1853.	Recog. to keep peace.
Wm. Patterson.	Larceny.	do	do	"	"	Convicted & sentenced 3 months imp. co jail.
Henry Smith,	Disorderly conduct.	do	do	"		Convicted, fined $5.
Darius Hill, Cyrus Hill & Henry Hill,	Resisting officer.	do	do	"		Under recog. to appear.
Cyrus Hill,	Assault with intent to kill.	do	do	"	March, 1853.	Recog. do
Darius Hill,	" "	do	do	"	"	No indictment found.
Nathan Smith,	Larceny.	do	do	"	"	Convicted, fined $5.
Henry S. Gifford,	Selling unwholesome provisions.	do	do	May, 1853.	"	Discontinued.
John P. and Abraham Johnson,	Malicious trespass.	do	do	"	"	Acquitted.
Ed B. Porter,	Having counterfeit bills in possession, with intent to pass the same.	do	do	"		Not disposed of—under recognizance.
Daniel W. VanArman,	Perjury.	do	do	June, 1853.	June, 1853.	Discharged.

Names	Offence charged	do			Remarks
Joseph C. Amsler	Passing counterfeit money.	do	"	June, 1855	Not disp. of, under recog.
Thomas McOmber	Malicious mischief	do	"		Discontinued
Elvis Arman	"	do	July, 1853	July, 1853	Conv'd, certiorari taken.
Jacob Halderman	Assault and battery	do	Sept., 1853		Not disp. of, under recog
Robert Wellwood	Obstructing railroad track.	do	Oct., "	Oct., 1853	Recog. forfeited—fled.
Jacob Wilderman	Passing counterfeit bills	do			Not disp. of, in custody
Gabriel Morehouse	"	do			" under recog.
Joseph C. Amsler and Gabriel Morehouse	Larceny	do	"		" in custody
John W. Davis	"	do	Nov., 1853	Nov., 1855	Convicted, 30 days imp
James Mahan	Assault and battery	do	"	"	" 50 "
Michael Gallagher	"	do	"	"	Discharged.
Mathew Egan	"	do	"	"	Convicted, fined $100.
Thomas Moran	"	do			

Branch County—JOHN G. PARKHURST, ESQ., *Prosecuting Attorney.*

CLASS I.—CASES PROSECUTED BY INDICTMENT.

Names of persons prosecuted.	Offence charged.	Month and year of indictment.	When disposed of.	How disposed of, punishment, if any, or present condition of the case.	Remarks
Abram Ackerson	Assault and battery.	Oct. 15, 1852	Dec., 1852	Tried and acquitted.	
Stephen Fowler	Assault with intent to kill	July, "	" "	Convicted.	Sentenced State prison 15 years
Rebecca Aldrich	Perjury.	Oct., "	" "	Nolle prosequi entered.	
Elea G. Parsons	Burglary.	June, 1851		Not disposed of.	
	Rape.	"		"	Tried twice; jury did not agree
Rebecca Aldrich	Perjury.	Oct., 1852		Not disposed of.	
William Eldrige	Assault and battery.	Dec., 1851		Continued for argument on special plea.	
Jarris Pierson	Misdemeanor.	June, "		Not disposed of.	
Jonas Y. Wood	Having counterfeit coin, with intent to pass the same.	Sept., 1852		"	
Robert Chaff	Assault and battery.	"		"	
Elmin Rumsey	Perjury.	"		"	
Jacob Grigg	"	"		"	
Silas N. Card	Nuisance.	"		"	

8

CLASS II.—CASES PROSECUTED OTHERWISE THAN BY INDICTMENT.

Names of persons prosecuted	Offence charged	Mode of prosecution.	In what court, whether before a justice or other magistrate.	When commenced	When disposed of	How disposed of, punishment, if any, or present condition of the case.
Martin Nichols & Joe: Sillernsey,	Assault and battery	Complaint.	Justice of the Peace.	Jan., 1853.	Jan., 1853.	Not guilty.
John Boys,	Larceny,	do	do	"	"	Guilty, 30 days in jail.
Martin and Levi Vail,		do	do			Disch'd; jury did'nt agree
Elisha Rumsey,	Perjury,	do	do	May, 1853	March, 1853.	Held to bail.
Jonas H & Levi Wood,	Counterfeiting.	do	do	May, 1853.		Guilty—county jail 10 dys and $25 fine
Timothy Clark,	Assault and battery.	do	do	May, 1853.		
Thomas Barrooke,	Larceny,	do	do	June, 1853.	May, 1853.	Jail 30 days, fined $5
John Byds,	Assault and battery.	do	do	"	June, 1853	Guilty—fined $5
Leonard Taylor,	"	do	do	July, 1853	July, 1853	Guilty, " $25.
Polly Williams,	Assault with intent to murder	do	do	"	"	Not guilty.
Phineas Mahlin, W. H Sprague and Robert Cluff,	"	do	do			Two first discharged, and Cluff held to bail
Elisha Fisher,	"	do	do			Not guilty.
Phebe Bennett,	Assault and battery.	do	do	Aug., 1853	Aug., 1853	Discharged.
Henry Bennett,	"	do	do	Oct., 1853.	Oct., 1853.	Guilty; Jail 2 dys, fine $10
Leamel H Rogers,	Arson.	do	do	"	"	Held to bail.
Elon G. Parsons,	False pretences	do	Circuit court court.	Nov., 1853.		Case continued

Calhoun County—D. DARWIN HUGHES, ESQ., Prosecuting Attorney.

CLASS I.—CASES PROSECUTED BY INDICTMENT.

Names of persons prosecuted.	Offence charged	Month and year of indictment.	When disposed of	How disposed of, punishment, if any, or present condition of the case.	Remarks
Baker Stillson,	Perjury,	Nov., 1849.		Not disposed of.	
Mary A. Smith,	"	"		"	
Eliza A. Pond,	"	"		"	
Calvin C. Burt,	Arson.	"		"	
Henry E and Charlotte Jones,	Malicious mischief.	Aug., 1850.		"	Filed
Alexander Moore.	False pretences.	May, 1851.		"	
Albert and Lerner Dunning,	Malicious mischief.	July, 1-52.		"	
Ab'm Come & Lyman Prichard,	Passing counterfeit money.	Oct., 1852.		"	
Abram Crane,	Having counterfeit money with intent to pass the same.	"		"	Filed.
Jesse Andrews,	Malicious mischief.	"		"	Under recognizance to appear.
Benjamin F. Burnett,	Libel.	Sept., 1853		"	

Names of persons prosecuted.	Offence charged.	Mode of prosecution.	In what court, whether before a justice or other magistrate.	When commenced.	When disposed of.	How disposed of, punishment, if any, or present condition of the case.
do	"	"			"	do
do	"	"			"	do
do	"	"			"	do
do	"	"			"	Fined $1 and 30 days imprisonment.
Charles Cowlan, William Jackson,	Compound larceny.	Convicted.			Sept., 1853.	Sentenced 5 years in State Prison.
do	Arson.	"			"	do
do	Perjury.	Not disposed of.			"	do
Thomas Dowling, Henry La-Grange, and Luke LaGrange,	Malicious mischief.					

CLASS II.—CASES PROSECUTED OTHERWISE THAN BY INDICTMENT.

Names of persons prosecuted.	Offence charged.	Mode of prosecution.	In what court, whether before a justice or other magistrate.	When commenced.	When disposed of.	How disposed of, punishment, if any, or present condition of the case.
Simon Aldrich,	Assault and battery.	Complaint.	Justice of the Peace.	Dec. 7, 1852	Dec. 7, 1852.	Conv'd, fine $3 & sureties.
Albert E. Langley,	"	do	do			" 30 days, county jail.
Stephen Hubbard,	"	do	do	Jan., 1853.	Jan., 1853.	" $15 fine.
Dennis Talbot,	Malicious mischief.	do	do	March, 1853.	March, 1853.	" 10 days, county jail.
Daniel Primdle,	Assault and battery.	do	do	"	"	" $5 fine.
John LaMunyon,	Disorderly person.	do	do			" recog. for 1 year.
Francis Ketchum,	Assault and battery.	do		May, 1853.	May, 1853.	" $1 fine.
Wm. A. Alvord,	Larceny.	Jury.	do	"	"	Acquitted.
James Case,	Common drunkard.	Complaint.	do			Convicted and committed for want of sureties.
Albert E. Langley,	"	do	do	June, 1853.	June, 1853.	Recog. for good behav'r.
Thomas Wixon,	Assault and battery.	do	do	"	"	Convicted, 3 months jail.
Stephen Wear,	Larceny.	do	do	"	"	"
Ganett VanKnocker,	Assault and battery.	do	do	"	"	10 days in jail.
John LaMunyon,	"	do	do	"	"	5 months in jail.
John O'Neal,	Disorderly person.	do	do			30 days jail, $5 fine.
John Bourk,	Assault and battery.	do	do	Aug., 1853.	Aug., 1853.	bound good behav'r.
Richard Martin,	A. assault and battery.	do	do	"	"	$3 fine.
Hiram Tyrrell,	Selling liquor.	do	do			$10 fine.
John G. Baker,	Threatening to beat, &c.	do	do	Oct., 1853.	Oct., 1853.	bound to k'p peace.
John D. Conkling,	Disorderly person.	do	do	Nov., 1853.	Nov., 1853.	commit'd for suret's
John Pottery,	"	do	do			bound good behav'r.
John Hyde,	Assault and battery.	Jury.	do	Dec., 1852.	Dec., 1852.	Settled.
James Maxley,	"	Complaint.	do	Jan., 1853.	Jan., 1853.	Convicted, 10 days in jail.
Martin Leach,	"	do	do	July, 1853.	July, 1853.	" $10 fine.
John McCaffey,	"	do	do	Aug., 1853.	Aug., 1853.	Acquitted.
Catharine McCaffey,	"	do	do			Convicted, $10 fine.
Horace C. Ladd,	"	do	do	Sept., 1853.	Sept., 1853.	Acquitted.
James Smith and George Hoyt,	Malicious trespass.	do	do	"	"	

CLASS II.—[CONTINUED.]

Names of persons prosecuted.	Offence charged.	Mode of prosecution.	In what court, whether before a justice of the peace or other magistrate.	When commenced.	When disposed of.	How disposed of, punishment, if any, or present condition of the case.
Charles H. Chotfee.	Assault and battery.	Complaint.	Justice of the Peace,	Oct., 1853.	Nov. 7, 1853.	Convicted, $3 fine.
Edward Wright.	Disorderly person.	do	do	Jan., 1853.	Jan., 1853.	" 15 days in jail.
Amos Taylor.	Larceny.	do	do	"		" $10 fine.
Harvey Shearman.	Assault and battery.	do	do	"		Settled.
Francis McCauley.	"	do	do	Feb., 1853.	Feb., 1853.	Convicted, $5 fine.
Patrick Kelly.	Disorderly person.	do	do	"	"	" conv'd for sureties.
Geo. W. Knox.	Assault and battery.	do	do			Not arrested.
Harvey Shearman.	"	do	do			"
Wm. H. Ella and Benj. Bailey.	Larceny.	do	do	March, 1853.	March, 1853.	Convicted, Ella 20 days in jail, Bailey $1 fine.
Jas. Lee.	Assault and battery.	do	do	"	"	Conv'l, 30 ds jail, $25 fine.
Wm. T. VanSickle.	"	do	do	"	"	Acquitted.
Henry Raymond.	"	do	do	April, 1853.	May, 1853.	Convicted, $10 fine.
Alonzo Cole.	"	do	do	Sept., 1853.	Sept., 1853.	" $3 fine.
Nelson Hall.	Threatening assault and battery.	do	do	Jan., 1853.	Jan., 1853.	Bound to keep peace.
Franklin Lucas.	Assault and battery.	do	do	June, 1853.	June, 1853.	Convicted, $1 fine.
Henry Luse.	"	do	do	Oct., 1853.	Oct., 1853.	" fined 25 cts & costs.
Miles Hall.	Threatening personal injury.	do	do			Bound to k'p peace 1 yr.
Frank Alberts.	Larceny.	do	do			Acquitted.
John Graham.	"	do	do	Nov., 1853.	Nov., 1853.	Withdrawn, (md. pros.)
Henry Wilcox.	"	do	do	May, 1853.	May, 1853.	Conv'd & in jail for trial.
Harmon M. Cornell.	"	do	do	March, 1853.	March, 1853.	Acquitted.
Joseph Scribner.	Disorderly person.	do	do	Jan., 1853.	Jan., 1853.	Convicted, fine $2 & costs.
William Casey.	"	do	do	"	"	"
Henry Lewis.	Assault and battery.	do	do	"	Feb., 1853.	" fined $5 and costs
William Toland.	"	do	do	"	Jan., 1853.	"
Geo. W. Munson.	Larceny.	do	do	May, 1853.	May, 1853.	" 30 days in jail.
Wm. Neal.	Assault and battery.	do	do	June, 1853.	June, 1853.	Acquitted.
Sidney R. Squires.	Assault and battery.	do	do			"
Levi Haskins.	Threatening to assault &c.	Jury.	do			
William C. Dumphrey, Byron Watkins & Charles Watkins.	Threatening to destroy property, &c.	Court.	do	July, 1853.	July, 1853.	R. Watkins b'nd k'p p'ce 6 mo., others disch'gd.
Lorenzo Coe.	False pretences.	"	do	Aug., 1853.	Sept., 1853.	Discharged.
Nathan Surrey.	Assault and battery.	"	do	April, 1853.		Acquitted.
Leonard Mills.	Larceny.	"	do	May, 1853.		Not arrested.
Abraham Woodbeck.	Assault and battery.		do	May, 1853.		"
William Estes.	Threat to kill.		do			"
Jackson Hodge & Wm. Bloom,	Disorderly persons.		do	Oct., 1853.		"
William Bloom and William						

			do	Dec., 1853.	....	"
Rayner,........	Assault with intent to kill.					
Moulton Thompson,........	Assault and battery.		do	Jan., 1853.	.... Jan., 1853.	Convicted, fined $50.

Cass County—HENRY H. COOLIDGE, ESQ., Prosecuting Attorney.

CLASS I.—CASES PROSECUTED BY INDICTMENT.

Names of persons prosecuted.	Offence charged.	Month and year of indictment.	When disposed of.	How disposed of, punishment, if any, or present condition of the case.	Remarks.
Samuel Smith,........	Malicious mischief.	Dec., 1852.	April, 1853.	Found guilty.	Sentenced to county jail 6 months.
David Kirk,........	Nuisance.	"		Not disposed of.	
Geo. Johnson,........	Compound larceny.	April, 1853.	April, 1853.	Guilty.	Sentenced to State Prison 3 years.
Jerry Van Arman and David	"		June, 1853.		Nolle prosequi.
Northrup,........	Burglary.	April, 1853.		Jury not able to agree.	
Daniel Keeney,........	Lewd and lascivious cohabitation.	June, 1853.		Case continued.	
Daniel S. Tollman,........	Assault with intent to kill.	"		Not disposed of.	
do	Larceny.	"		do	
John Smith,........		"		do	

CLASS II.—CASES PROSECUTED OTHERWISE THAN BY INDICTMENT.

Names of persons prosecuted.	Offence charged.	Mode of prosecution.	In what court, whether before a justice or other magistrate.	When commenced.	When disposed of.	How disposed of, punishment, if any, or present condition of the case.	Remarks.
David & Eliza Beardsley,........	Assault and battery.	Complaint.	Justice of the Peace.	March, 1853.	March, 1853.	Not guilty.	
Benjamin Wyneous,........	Larceny.	"	"	June, 1853.	June, 1853.	Guilty, fined $100.	
Joseph Shanahoe,........	Assault and battery.	"	"	Nov., 1853.	Nov., 1853.	" $50.	
John Rosevelt,........	do	"	"	Oct., 1853.	Oct., 1853.	" $15.	

Clinton County—R. STRICKLAND, ESQ., Prosecuting Attorney.

CLASS I.—CASES PROSECUTED BY INDICTMENT.

Names of persons prosecuted.	Offence charged.	Month and year of indictment.	When disposed of.	How disposed of, punishment, if any, or present condition of the case.	Remarks.
William Letts,........	Malicious mischief.	June, 1853.	June, 1853.	Guilty.	Removed to Supreme Court.
Nelson J. Allport,........	False pretences.	"		Not disposed of.	
John Park,........	Larceny.	"		"	
Rufus Briggs,........	Assault and battery.	"		"	
Gardner Chappell,........	Crime against nature.	"		"	
Rufus Briggs,........	Assault and battery.	"		"	

CLASS II.—CASES PROSECUTED OTHERWISE THAN BY INDICTMENT.

Names of persons prosecuted.	Offence charged.	Mode of prosecution.	In what court, whether before a justice or other magistrate.	When commenced.	When disposed of.	How disposed of, punishment, if any, or present condition of the case.
A. E. Bryant,	Assault and battery.	Complaint.	Justice of the Peace.	Aug., 1853.	Aug., 1853.	Guilty—fined $35.
William Letts,	Larceny.	do	do	" "	" "	" " $30.
E. Rose,	Assault and battery.	do	do	Sept., 1853.	Sept., 1853.	" " $15.
S. Brass,	Selling liquor.	do	do	" "	" "	" " $25.
Thomas Wilson,	Assault and battery.	do	do	Nov., 1853.	Nov., 1853.	" " $15.
do	Disturbing religious meeting.	do	do	" "	" "	" " $10.

Eaton County—M. S. BRACKETT, Esq., *Prosecuting Attorney.*

CLASS I.—CASES PROSECUTED BY INDICTMENT.

Names of persons prosecuted.	Offence charged.	Month and year of indictment.	When disposed of.	How disposed of, punishment, if any, or present condition of the case.	Remarks.
Henry A. Shaw,	Assault and battery.	Nov., 1853.		Not disposed of.	
do	Maintainance.	"		"	

CLASS II.—CASES PROSECUTED OTHERWISE THAN BY INDICTMENT.

Names of persons prosecuted	Offence charged	Mode of prosecution.	In what court, whether before a justice or other magistrate.	When commenced	When disposed of.	How disposed of, punishment, if any, or present condition of the case.
William Otis,	Larceny.	Complaint.	Justice of the Peace.	Dec., 1852.	Dec., 1852.	Escaped during trial.
Palmer Tenga,	Perjury.	do	do	March, 1853.	March, 1853.	Held to bail.
Eliza Bond,	Assault and battery,	do	do	"	"	Settled.
Manlius Mann,	Trespass on State lands	do	do			
Earl Horsington, Chester Horsington, Orrin A Horsington,	Larceny.	do	do	April, 1853.	April, 1853.	Three trials—discharged.
Philleman Nettleton,	Assault and battery.	do	do	"	"	Guilty—fined $15.
Joseph Mills,	Rape.	do	do	"	"	Held to bail—escaped.

Genesee County—A. P. DAVIS, ESQ., Prosecuting Attorney.

CLASS I.—CASES PROSECUTED BY INDICTMENT.

Names of persons prosecuted.	Offence charged.	Month and year of indictment.	When disposed of.	How disposed of, punishment, if any, or present condition of the case.	Remarks.
Timothy J. Tucker,	Malicious mischief.	April, 1853.		Not disposed of.	
Isaac Power,	Passing counterfeit money.	"		"	
Joshua C. Corwin,	Grand larceny.	"		"	
Adam J. Worth and James Sisco,					Indictment quashed.
Augustus St. Armand,	False pretences.	"	Sept., 1853.	Discharged.	
Alvah E. Powelson,	Embezzlement.	"		Not disposed of.	
Albert Powelson,	Assault with intent to kill.	"			
Joseph McNamee,	Accessory to do	"			
Henry Johnson,	Selling unwholesome provisions.	"	June, 1853.	Convicted.	
William P. Bailey,	Embezzlement.	"	"	Discharged.	
do	Extortion.	"	"	Acquitted.	New trial granted.
William Bates,	Arson.	Sept., 1853.	Oct., 1853.	Convicted.	"

CLASS II.—CASES PROSECUTED OTHERWISE THAN BY INDICTMENT.

Names of persons prosecuted	Offence charged.	Mode of prosecution.	In what court, whether before a justice or other magistrate.	When commenced	When disposed of.	How disposed of, punishment, if any, or present condition of the case.
Peter Waters,	Assault and battery.	Warrant.	Justice of the Peace.	Dec., 1852.	Dec., 1852.	Fined $5; committed
John McEwen,	"	do	do			" $30; com'd, disch'd on habeas corpus.
William Pratt,	Larceny.	do	do	March, 1853.	March, 1853.	Fined; in default impris'd.
Christian Wenzer,	Disorderly person.	do	do	July, 1853.	July, 1853.	Bound to keep the peace.
William Morrison,	Larceny.	do	do	Nov., 1853.	Nov., 1853.	Imprisoned.
Manly Rump,	Assault and battery.	do	do	Oct., 1853.	Oct., 1853.	Fined $10—fine paid.
Avra Bradley,	"	do	do	Dec., 1852.	Dec., 1852.	Fined—paid fine.
Robert McCowen,	Obtaining goods under false pretences.	do	do	Jan., 1853.	Jan., 1853	Recognized to court.
James Cramer,	Assault and battery.	do	do	Feb., 1853.	Feb., 1853.	Verdict not guilty.
Michael Murphy,	Disorderly person.	do	do	June, 1853.	June, 1853.	Recog. to keep the peace.
George Drain,	Assault with intent to kill.	do	do	July, 1853.	July, 1853.	Recognized to court.
Henry Hollabander,	Assault and battery.	do	do	Aug., 1853.	Aug., 1853.	Verdict not guilty.
George Drain,	Disorderly person.	do	do	"	"	Recog. to keep the peace.
John Hilburd, Jr.	"	do	do	Sept., 1853.	Sept., 1853.	do
Hinker Hibbard,	"	do	do	"	"	do
Isaac Powers,	Passing counterfeit money.	do	do	Dec., 1852.	Dec., 1852.	Recog. to circuit court.

CLASS II.—[CONTINUED.]

Names of persons prosecuted.	Offence charged.	Mode of prosecution.	In what court, whether before a justice or other magistrate.	When commenced.	When disposed of.	How disposed of, punishment, if any, or present condition of the case.
Isaac A. Worden,	Assault and battery.	Warrant	Justice of the Peace.	Jan., 1853.	Jan., 1853.	Discharged.
Robert Cowen,	Larceny.	do	do	"	Feb., 1853.	Fined.
William T. Hill,	Assault and battery.	do	do	Feb., 1853.	March, 1853.	Recog. to circuit court.
Charles Richmond,	Obtaining goods under false pretences.	do	do	"	May, 1853.	Discharged.
Mary Quin,	"	do	do	April, 1853.	Aug., 1853.	Fined.
William Meecham,	Assault and battery.	do	do	Aug., 1853.	Sept., 1853.	Committed for trial.
William Bates,	Arson.	do	do	Sept., 1853.	Sept., 1853.	Dismissed.
George L. Martin,	Larceny.	do	do	Aug., 1853.	Aug., 1853.	Discharged.
George Bevins,	"	do	do			

Hillsdale County—E. H. Wilson, Esq., Prosecuting Attorney.

CLASS I.—CASES PROSECUTED BY INDICTMENT.

Names of persons prosecuted.	Offence charged.	Month and year of indictment.	When disposed of.	How disposed of, punishment, if any, or present condition of the case.	Remarks.
Oliver Clark,	Passing counterfeit bills.	April, 1852.		Not disposed of.	
Sherburne Gaige,	Perjury.	"		"	
James A. Salloway,	"	"		"	
William C. Richards,	"	"		"	
Augustus Finney,	False pretences.	"		"	
John Bigelow,	Malicious mischief.	"		"	
James Burdell,	Larceny.	"		"	
John Griffith,	"	"		"	
Franklin Crandall,	"	"	April, 1853.	Acquitted.	
Harriet R. Galloway,	Assault with intent to kill.	"	"	"	
Thomas Fowler,	Larceny.	"	"	"	
Leonard Billy, Robert Billy and Abram VanAlstine,	Misdemeanor.	"	"	"	
Solomon Oaks,	"	"	"	Not disposed of.	
do	"	"		"	
Thomas Billy,	Assault and battery.	"		Acquitted.	
Samuel Billy,	"	"		"	
Oliver Clark,	Passing counterfeit money.	"		Not disposed of.	
Augustus Finney,	Larceny.	"		"	
Peter Smith,	"	Nov., 1852.	Nov., 1852.	Convicted.	Sentenced State prison 4 years.
Hiram Correll,	"	"	"	"	"

Names of persons prosecuted.	Offence charged.	When commenced.	When disposed of.	How disposed of, punishment, if any, or present condition of the case.
Marshall Chilson,	False pretences.			"
Henry B. Williams,	"			"
Jonas W. Wood,	"		Not disposed of.	3
Orren Stanbro,	Assault with intent to kill.		"	
William Knickerbocker,	Burglary.		"	
David Smith,	Larceny.		"	
Seth English,	False pretences.		"	
John Kelly, et al,	Riot.	Nov., 1853.	"	Absconded.
Mezes Leder,	Burglary.		"	
Thomas Billy,	Assault and battery.			
Samuel Billy,	"	April, 1853.	Nov., 1853.	Convicted. Sentenced to State prison 5 years.
Milo Hawley, et al,	Riot.	"	April, 1853.	Acquitted.
Barney Reynolds,	Assault with intent to kill.	"	"	Convicted. Fined $20 each.
William Beckwith, et al,	Riot.	Nov., 1853.	Nov., 1853.	Convicted. Not disposed of.

CLASS II.—CASES PROSECUTED OTHERWISE THAN BY INDICTMENT.

Names of persons prosecuted.	Offence charged.	Mode of prosecution.	In what court, whether before a justice or other magistrate.	When commenced.	When disposed of.	How disposed of, punishment, if any, or present condition of the case.
Ambrose Fish,	Larceny.	Complaint.	Justice of the Peace.	Dec., 1852.	Dec., 1852.	Recognized.
Alanson Trumbull,	Assault and battery.	do	do	"	"	Discharged.
Orrin Everett,	"	do	do	"	"	"
Barton Tiffany,	"	do	do	"	"	"
Sheldon Smith,	"	do	do	Jan., 1853.	Jan., 1853.	"
John Maguire,	Adultery.	do	do	"	"	Recognized.
John Bigelow,	Malicious mischief.	do	do	"	"	"
Augustus Timerly,	False pretences.	do	do	"	"	"
John Kelly,		do	do	"	"	"
Alfred J. Powers,	Larceny.	do	do	"	"	Convicted.
Thomas Tenny,	Assault and battery.	do	do	"	"	Order to recognize.
Wm. P. Richards,	Perjury.	do	do	"	"	Recog. to keep peace.
Myron Van Alstine,	Threats.	do	do	Feb., 1853.	Feb., 1853.	Paid costs—not, pros.
Jerome Burroughs,	Fraud.	do	do	Jan., 1853.	Jan., 1853.	Dismissed.
Uriah B. Couch,	Assault and battery.	do	do		Feb., 1853.	Acquitted.
Chas. & Abram Van Alstine,	"	do	do	Feb., 1853.		Fined $28—appealed
Elias G. Dills,	"	do	do	"		Acquitted by jury.
Timothy Baker,		do	do		March, 1863.	Bound to circuit court.
Harriet R. Galloway,	Administering poison.	do	do	March, 1853.		
Wm. Jackson,	Larceny.	do	do	April, 1853.	April, 1853.	Convicted and fined $10.
John Collan,	Assault and battery.	do	do	"	"	Recog. to keep peace.
John Weatherway,	Threats.	do	do			Bound to circuit court
Morris A. Yates,	Fraud.	do	do		May, 1853.	
Augustus Lane, et al,	Obstructing an officer.	do	do	May, 1853	"	

CLASS II.—[CONTINUED.]

Names of persons prosecuted.	Offence charged.	Mode of prosecution.	In what court, whether before a justice or other magistrate.	When commenced.	When disposed of.	How disposed of, punishment, if any, or present condition of the case.
Henry Whitehead,	Assault and battery.	Complaint.	Justice of the Peace.	June, 1853.	June, 1853	Acquitted.
John Ostrander,		do	do		July, "	Settled and costs paid.
Barney Reynolds,	Assault with intent to kill.	do	do			Bound to circuit court.
Henry B. Williams, Jonas W. Wood,		do	do	July, 1853.	" "	"
Kman Baker,	Fraud.	do	do			Acquitted by Jury.
Hiram Covill, Marshall Chilison,	Assault and battery.	do	do			"
Henry Covill,	Larceny.	do	do	Sept., 1853	Sept., 1853	Bound to circuit court.
Henry Crandall,	Threats.	do	do	Oct., 1853.	Oct., 1853	Recog. to keep peace.
Alpheus B. Hill,	Fraud.	do	do			No return on warrant.
John Bartow,	Threats.	do	do	Nov., 1853	Nov., 1853.	Recog to keep peace.
Dewitt C. Button,	Seduction.	do	do			Bound to circuit court

Ingham County—ORLANDO M. BARNES, ESQ., Prosecuting Attorney.

CLASS I.—CASES PROSECUTED BY INDICTMENT.

Names of persons prosecuted.	Offence charged.	Month and year of indictment.	When disposed of.	How disposed of, punishment, if any, or present condition of the case.	Remarks.
William Megiveron,	Assault and battery.	1849.		Not disposed of.	
Fayette Baldwin,	Larceny.	Sept., 1851.	Oct., 1853.	Nolle prosequi.	
Crandall M. Howard,	Perjury.			Not disposed of.	
James Dakin,	Rape.	May, 1852.		Recognizance forfeited.	
Palmer Rossman,	Escape.	" "	Oct., 1853,	Acquitted.	
Horace Havens,	False pretences.			Recognizance forfeited.	
Ruel Blakealey,	"			Not disposed of.	
James Hitchcock,	Murder.	May, 1853.	May, 1853.	Convicted of murder in the first degree.	Sentenced to State Prison for life.
John G. Johnson,	False pretences.	"	Oct., 1852.	Nolle prosequi.	Settled.

CLASS II.—CASES PROSECUTED OTHERWISE THAN BY INDICTMENT.

Names of persons prosecuted.	Offence charged.	Mode of prosecution.	In what court, whether before a justice or other magistrate.	When commenced.	When disposed of.	How disposed of, punishment, if any, or present condition of the case.
Hiram Baker,	Disorderly conduct.		Justice of the Peace.	Dec., 1852.	Dec., 1852.	Fined $4.
Geo. Carmer,	"		do	" "	" "	

Ionia County—John C. Blanchard, Esq., *Prosecuting Attorney.*

CLASS I.—CASES PROSECUTED BY INDICTMENT.

Names of persons prosecuted	Offence charged	Month and year of indictment	When disposed of	How disposed of, punishment, if any, or present condition of the case	Remarks
—— Dean,	Assault and battery.	Jan., 1853.	Jan., 1853.	Acquitted.	
—— Trefry,	Disorderly conduct.	Feb., 1853.	Feb., "	Discontinued.	
T. Montgomery,	Assault and battery.	"	"	Fined $10.	
Wilbur Earl,	"	March, 1853.	April, 1853.	Convicted and fined $15.	
David Dean,	"	"	March, 1863.	Tried and imprisoned.	
Moses H. White,	Fraud.	"	"	acquitted.	
F. White,	Assault and battery.	April, 1853.	April, 1853.	convicted.	
John Winkley,	Larceny.	May, 1853.	May, 1853.	Convicted, fined $5.	
Eli Campbell,	"	Aug., 1853.	Aug., 1853.	fine $15.	
J. Hudson,	Assault and battery.	Nov., 1853.	Nov., 1853.	fined $12.	
C. A. Osborn,	"				
Zina Loyd,	Assault and battery.	April, 1853.		Not disposed of.	
Jefferson Bennett,	Passing counterfeit bills.	"			Defendant ran away.
Harry Wilder,	Compound larceny.	"			"
Benjamin Childester,	Seduction.				
Hosmer Bement,	Perjury.	Oct., 1853.	Oct., 1853.	Acquitted.	
do	Adultery.	"		Not disposed of.	
Susan Meginley,	Bigamy.	"			

CLASS II.—CASES PROSECUTED OTHERWISE THAN BY INDICTMENT.

Names of persons prosecuted	Offence charged	Mode of prosecution.	In what court, whether before a justice or other magistrate.	When commenced.	When disposed of.	How disposed of, punishment, if any, or present condition of the case.
James Bliss,	Malicious mischief.	Complaint.	Justice of the Peace.	Feb., 1853.	Feb., 1853.	Guilty, jail 15 days.
James Stearns,	Larceny.	do	do	April, 1853.		" fined $25.
Darius Dodge,	Assault and battery.	do	do	Oct.,		" fined $5.

Jackson County—AUSTIN BLAIR, Esq., *Prosecuting Attorney.*

CLASS I.—CASES PROSECUTED BY INDICTMENT.

Names of persons prosecuted.	Offence charged.	Month and year of indictment.	When disposed of.	How disposed of, punishment, if any, or present condition of the case.	Remarks.
James L. Smalley,	Larceny.	June, 1853.		Recognizance forfeited.	Fled.
Charles Graham,	"	"	Sept., 1853.	Nolle prosequi.	Recaped.
Hiram G. Davis,	"			Not disposed of.	
John Pettis,	"			"	
Lorenzo Badgley,	Assault and battery.	Nov., 1853.	Nov., 1853.	Nolle prosequi.	Settled.
Morris Ready and Bridget Donahue,	Lewd conduct.	"		Convicted.	Fined $27 and committed to jail.
William J. Crout,	Trespass on State lands	"		Not disposed of.	
Lewis Badgley, James Bates and Haley Winans,	Assault and battery.	"		"	
Amos Cozin,	Embezzlement.	"			
George Wells,	Larceny.	"	March, 1853.	Convicted.	Sentenced to State Prison 3 years.
Benjamin F. Emerson,	Perjury.	"	June, 1853.	Nolle prosequi.	
Benjamin Gordon,	Resisting officer.	"	Nov., 1853.	"	
Phebe Gordon.	"			"	
Cyrenus Gordon,	Larceny.	June, 1853.	June, 1853.	Convicted.	Sentenced to State prison 2 years.
William Collins,	"	"	"	"	" 1 year.
Charles Daly,	"	"		"	
David Daly,	"	"		Acquitted.	

CLASS II.—CASES PROSECUTED OTHERWISE THAN BY INDICTMENT.

Names of persons prosecuted	Offence charged.	Mode of prosecution.	In what court, whether before a justice or other magistrate.	When commenced.	When disposed of.	How disposed of, punishment, if any, or present condition of the case.
Owen Ellison,	Assault and battery.	Complaint.	Justice of the Peace.	April, 1853.	May, 1853.	Convicted, fine $5.
Owen Ellison, jr.,	"	do	do	"	"	$1 fine.
Whitfield Ellison,	"	do	do	"	"	$1 fine.
Lewis Badgley,	"	do	do	Jan., 1853.	Feb., 1853.	$4 fine.
George Putner,	"	do	do	May, 1853.	June, 1853.	$3 fine.
Lawrence Ryan,	"	do	do	March, 1853.	April, 1853.	$5 fine.
Patrick McFallen,	"	do	do	Dec., 1853.	Jan., 1853	$10 fine.
Nathan Haskell,	"	do	do	Aug., 1853.	Sept., 1853.	$25 fine.
Wilson J. Matthews,	"	do	do			Acquitted.
Joshua Garvell,	"	do,	do	July, 1853.	July, 1853.	Convicted, $12 fine.
Edward J. Constable,	"	do,	do	"	"	$20 fine.

Lapeer County—JOHN M. WATTLES, Esq., *Prosecuting Attorney.*

Names of persons prosecuted	Offence charged	Month and year of indictment	When disposed of	Remarks
William S. Warner	"		"	fine $8.
Ami Collins	"	June, 1853	June, 1853	fine $10.
Lewis Post	"	Jan., 1853.	Jan., 1853.	fine $3.
Daniel B. Hibbard	"	Feb., 1853.	Feb., 1853.	fine $5.
Nicholas Huffaling	"	Jan., 1853.	Jan., 1853.	fine $25.
George Hawkins	"	Nov., 1852.	Dec., 1852.	"
Victor T. Dutton	"	Dec., 1852.	Dec., 1852.	fine $15.
James Secord	"			fine $10.
Ira W. Kellogg	"			fine $15.
Thomas Blair	"	Sept., 1853.	Sept., 1853.	fine $3.
James Green	"	Oct., 1853.	Nov., 1853.	fine $25.
Michael Kelly	Threats of violence.	Nov., 1853.		10 dys imp., and fine $5.
Conrad Aich	Disorderly conduct.	Dec., 1853.	Dec., 1853.	Recog. to keep peace.
Daniel Kelahee	Contempt of court.	Nov., 1853.	Nov., 1853.	Convicted, fine $1.
do	Larceny.			" fine $5.
Gilbert Dunn	do	Dec., 1852.	Dec., 1852.	Sentenced 30 days imp.
Joelton G. Havens	"	June, 1853.	July, 1853.	Convicted, fine $12.
Amos Howe	"	Sept., 1853.	Sept., 1853.	" fine $6.
William Jones	"			" fine $8.
Simon Peter Wyskoff	"			" fine $5
Henry Chapman	"	May, 1853.	May, 1853.	Sentenced 20 days imp., and fined $10.
George Wells	Disorderly conduct.	March, 1853.	April, 1853.	30 days imp., and fine $8.
Harper Morrill	"	July, 1853.	July, 1853.	Acquitted.

CLASS I.—CASES PROSECUTED BY INDICTMENT.

Names of persons prosecuted	Offence charged	Month and year of indictment	When disposed of	How disposed of, punishment, if any, or present condition of the case.	Remarks
Jarod L. Phile	Assault with intent to kill.	May, 1853.	....	Not disposed of.	
John Warren	Larceny.	"	....	"	
Phillip Hartwell	"	Oct., 1853.	....	"	

CLASS II.—CASES PROSECUTED OTHERWISE THAN BY INDICTMENT.

Names of persons prosecuted.	Offence charged.	Mode of prosecution.	In what court, whether before a Justice or other magistrate.	When commenced.	When disposed of.	How disposed of, punishment, if any, or present condition of the case.
John S. Fellards,	Larceny.	Complaint.	Justice of the Peace.	Jan., 1853.	Jan., 1853.	Convicted, fined $25.
Wm. S. Graves,	Assault and battery.	do	do	March, 1853.	March, 1853.	" " $3.
Stephen V. Warren,	"	do	do	"	"	" " $10.
Stephen Tuttle,	"	do	do	Sept., 1853.	Sept., 1853.	" " $3.
Thomas Walker,	"	do	do	Nov., 1853.	Nov., 1853.	" " $9.

Lenawee County—SMITH M. WILKINSON, Esq., Prosecuting Attorney.

CLASS I.—CASES PROSECUTED BY INDICTMENT.

Names of persons prosecuted.	Offence charged.	Month and year of indictment.	When disposed of.	How disposed of, punishment, if any, or present condition of the case.	Remarks.
Moses S. Chamberlin,	Perjury.	Mar., 1852.	March, 1852.	Still pending.	Not arrested.
Seth P. Bascomy,	Larceny.	"	"	"	do
do	Assault with intent to kill.	"	"	"	do
do	Receiving stolen goods.	"	"	"	do
do	Larceny.	"	"	"	do
Seymour Van Syckle,	Malicious trespass.	"	"	"	Under Recognizance.
James Allen,	Incest.	"	"	"	Not arrested.
George Hall,	Burglary and Larceny.	"	"	"	Escaped.
John Brown,	"	"	"	"	
Samuel Chadwick,	"	Sept., 1852.	March, 1853.	Nolle Presequi.	
do	Assault with intent to commit rape.	"	"	Still pending.	Not arrested.
Henry Tubbs,	Forgery.	March, 1852.	"	Convicted.	Sentenced to State Prison 2 years.
Lyman Nelson,	Assault with intent to kill.	"	"	"	do
John Green,	Larceny.	"	"	Nel. Pros.	
Samuel Chadwick,	Perjury.	Sept., 1853.	"	"	
David T. Lowe,	Forgery.	"	"	Convicted.	Jury disagreed on trial.
James L. Peeking,	Forgery.	"	"	Nol. Pros.	do
Franklin Beckwith,	Larceny.				Sentenced 4 years to State Prison.

CLASS II.—CASES PROSECUTED OTHERWISE THAN BY INDICTMENT.

Names of persons prosecuted.	Offence charged.	Mode of prosecution.	In what court, whether before a justice or other magistrate.	When commenced.	When disposed of.	How disposed of, punishment, if any, or present condition of the case.
Peter Keller	Bastardy.	Complaint.	Justice of the Peace.	July, 1853	July, 1853.	Defend't died before trial.
John Corey	Larceny.	do	do	Dec., 1852	Dec., 1852.	Carv'd, 30 ds ;1 $10 fine
Charles Rudolph	Assault and battery.	do	do	"	"	Fined $10.
John Green	"	do	do	May, 1853	May, 1853.	5.
Alvin Porter	"	do	do	Sept., 1853	Sept., 1853.	5.
Jesse Osborn	"	do	do	Mar., 1853	March, 1853.	15.
Thomas S. Williams	"	do	do	Feb., 1853	Feb., 1853.	10.
Richard Clegg	Larceny.	do	do	"	"	10.
Thomas S. Williams	"	do	do	May, 1853	May, 1853.	to Co. ;1 60 ds.
John Eisenhard	"	do	do	"	"	
Landis Roode	"	do	do	July, 1853	July, 1853.	Sentenced 10 da co tt
Michael Elliott	"	do	do	May, 1853	May, 1853	Acquitted.
Mathis Dalley	Assault and battery.	do	do	June, 1853	June, 1853	Fined $5.
Ezekiel Shumway	"	do	do	"	"	Fined $10.
George L. Hathaway	"	do	do	"	"	Acquitted.
James Kelley	"	dn	do	Sept., 1853	Sept., 1853.	Fined $7.
Daniel Brayman	"	do	do	Oct., 1853	Oct., 1853.	$10 fine, co. ;1 10 ds.
James Riley	"	do	do	Nov., 1853	Nov., 1853.	do do 8
John Schnell	"	do	do	"	"	Bound to circuit court.
Gregory Ulrich	Seduction.	do	dn	"	"	Bound to circuit court.
Edmond Grandy	Larceny.	do	do	"	"	Judg't against def't $25
Darius Sherman	Selling liquor.	do	do	June, 1853.	June, 1853.	Fined $5.
Joseph Bowers	Malicious mischief.	Debt.	do	May, 1853.	May, 1853.	
James Myers		Complaint.				

Livingston County—W. A. CLARK, ESQ., *Prosecuting Attorney.*

CLASS I.—CASES PROSECUTED BY INDICTMENT.

Names of persons prosecuted.	Offence charged.	Month and year of indictment.	When disposed of.	How disposed of, punishment, if any, or present condition of the case.	Remarks.
Elijah Roof	Extortion.	April, 1853.	April, 1853.	Acquitted.	
Elijah Badgero	Burglary.	Aug., 1852.	Aug., 1853.	Convicted.	Sentenced State prison 7 years

CLASS II.—CASES PROSECUTED OTHERWISE THAN BY INDICTMENT.

Names of persons prosecuted	Offence charged.	Mode of prosecution.	In what court, whether before a justice or other magistrate.	When commenced.	When disposed of.	How disposed of, punishment, if any, or present condition of the case.
John Doe,	Larceny.	Complaint.	Justice of the Peace.	July, 1853.	July, 1853.	Guilty, 20 days in jail.
Robert Graham,	Assault and battery.	do	do	Sept., 1853.	Sept., 1853.	3 mos. in jail, fine $100
John Jordan,	Malicious injury.	do	do	Aug., 1853.	Aug., 1853.	Guilty, 10 days in jail
Joseph Griswold,	"	do	do	"	"	do
Asa McFall,	Larceny.	do	do			fined $20.
Israel Ferguson,	Threats.	do	do	Sept., 1853.	Sept., 1853.	Gave bail to keep peace.
William Waits & Obed Power,	Assault and battery.	do	do	"	"	Guilty, fined $5.
James Griffiths.	Malicious injury.	do	do	July, "	Nov., 1853.	" fined.
Michael Mason,	Larceny.	do	do	May, 1853.	May, 1853.	" 30 days in jail
Aaron Munroe,	Assault and battery.	do	do	Oct., 1852.		" fined $10.

Macomb County—GILES HUBBARD, ESQ., *Prosecuting Attorney.*

No Indictments found for the year ending November 30, 1853, in this county.

CLASS II.—CASES PROSECUTED OTHERWISE THAN BY INDICTMENT.

Names of persons prosecuted	Offence charged.	Mode of prosecution.	In what court, whether before a justice or other magistrate.	When commenced.	When disposed of.	How disposed of, punishment, if any, or present condition of the case.
James Kelly.	Assault and battery.	Complaint.	Justice of the Peace.	Dec., 1852.	Jan., 1853.	Fined.
Francis Bluy,	Larceny.	do	do	March, 1853.	March, 1853.	Discharged.
Clement Bluy,	"	do	do	"		
George Nichols,	Assault and battery.	do	do			Fined
John O'Neil,	"	do	do	April, 1853.	April, 1853.	Settled.
do	"	do	do			Not arrested
Joseph D. Godfry,	Disorderly conduct.	do	do	May, 1853.	May, 1853.	Imprisoned 10 dys in jail.
Charles Dabo,	Assault and battery.	do	do	"		Not arrested
Benjamin Bates,	"	do	do	Sept., 1853.		Settled.
Oliver Beach,	"	do	do	"		"
John and Peter Gilbert,	"	do	do			Discharged.
Frederick Harter,	"	do	do	Oct., 1853.		"
Gilbert Bates,	"	do	do	Nov., 1853.		Fined
John Worden,	"	do	do			

Monroe County—JUNIUS TILDEN, ESQ., Prosecuting Attorney.

CLASS I.—CASES PROSECUTED BY INDICTMENT.

Names of persons prosecuted.	Offence charged.	Month and year of indictment.	When disposed of.	How disposed of, punishment, if any, or present condition of the case.	Remarks.
Charles F. Grobe,	Larceny.	June, 1852.	Dec., 1852.	Acquitted.	
Albert Cole, et al,	Robbery.	Dec., 1852.	March, 1853.	"	Sentenced 3 years in State Prison.
Marcus Beeler,	Larceny.	"	"	Convicted.	
Lewis Lambart,	Seduction.	March 1853		Not disposed of.	
Joseph Benani, Jr.,	Larceny.	"	March, 1853.	Convicted.	Sentenced 30 days county jail.
James A. Downrathy,	Assault and battery.	"	"	Acquitted.	
Silas W. Eaton,	Escape.	"	"	Convicted.	Fined $10 and costs.
James S. Donavee,	Larceny.	June, 1853.	June, 1853.	"	Sentenced to county jail 6 months.
Alexander McIntyre and Samuel Russ,	Nuisance.	"		Not disposed of.	
Robert H. Calkins,	"	"		"	
Edward Loranger,	"	"		"	
John J Chamberlin and James M. Chamberlin,	"	"			

CLASS II.—CASES PROSECUTED OTHERWISE THAN BY INDICTMENT.

Names of persons prosecuted.	Offence charged.	Mode of prosecution.	In what court, whether before a justice or other magistrate.	When commenced.	When disposed of.	How disposed of, punishment, if any, or present condition of the case.
Isidore Peltier,	Disorderly person.	Warrant.	Justice of the Peace.	Nov., 1852.		Entered recognisance.
Alexander Cousineau,	Threats.	do	do	"		"
David Hutchins,	Larceny.	do	do	"		Not guilty.
John Knoll,	Disorderly conduct.	do	do	"		Guilty, fined $5.
Oliver Stewart,	Assault and battery.	do	do	Jan., 1853.		" "
John E. Hammel,	"	do	do	"		" "
George Philips,	"	do	do	"		Not guilty.
Barnard Hurty,	Disorderly conduct.	do	do	March, 1853.		Fined 50 cents.
Henry Hale,	Assault and battery.	do	do	"		" $3.
Alexander LaCadie,	"	do	do	"		" $5, impris'd 10 dys.
Patrick Cinlon,	"	do	do	"		" $5.
Jarvis Eldred,	"	do	do	"		" $3.
John E. Hammel,	Threats.	do	do	April, 1853.		Three dys imprisonment.
Alanson Cooley,	"	do	do	"		Entered recognisance.
Isidore Peltier,	Disorderly conduct.	do	do	"		"

CLASS II.—[CONTINUED.]

Names of persons prosecuted.	Offence charged.	Mode of prosecution.	In what court, whether before a justice or other magistrate.	When commenced.	When disposed of.	How disposed of, punishment, if any, or present condition of the case.
Allen Piquet	Assault and battery.	Warrant.	Justice of the Peace.	May, 1853.	----	Fined $10.
David Savage	"	do	do	"	----	" $3.
William Howell	"	do	do	"	----	" $10.
James Murphy	Disorderly conduct.	do	do	June, 1853.	----	Entered recognizance.
John Walker	Larceny.	do	do	July, 1853.	----	Ten days imprisonment.
Charles B. Weaver	Assault and battery.	do	do	"	----	Fined $10.
John Halbeg	Disorderly conduct.	do	do	"	----	Not guilty.
Charles Beerman	Assault and battery.	do	dn	"	----	Fined $1.
Michael Kitty	"	do	do	Sept., 1853.	----	Imp. 30 days, fined $20
John Menard	Larceny.	do	do	"	----	" 10 " $5
Thomas Keegan	Assault and battery.	do	do	"	----	Fined $9.
James Peare	"	do	do	"	----	Fined $3.
Frederick Uhlendorf	Selling liquor without license.	Summons.	do	"	----	Penalty imposed $25.
Peter Nufer	"	do	do	"	----	$10.
James Murphy	"	do	do	"	----	$25.
John Johnson	Obstruction of highway.	do	do	Oct., 1853.	----	$20.

Oakland County.—AUG. C. BALDWIN, Esq., Prosecuting Attorney.

CLASS I.—CASES PROSECUTED BY INDICTMENT.

Names of persons prosecuted.	Offence charged.	Month and year of indictment.	When disposed of.	How disposed of, punishment, if any, or present condition of the case.	Remarks.
John Hughes	Assault and battery.	Oct., 1850.	Oct., 1853.	Convicted.	
Ann Williams	"	Oct., 1853.	April, 1853.	"	
Philo Williams	"	"	"		
Eugene Clark	Illegal voting	April, 1853.	June, 1853.	Convicted.	
John Lyster	"	"	"	2 trials; jury not agreeing	
David Lyster	"	"	"	Not disposed of.	
Joseph C. Lyster				"	
Thomas Lyon, Noah Goulds, Morris Goulds, David Goulds, Hugh Van Gordon	Larceny	"	"	"	
Joseph Gray	Trespass on State lands				
Charles Hannibal, Elizabeth Hannibal, Hannah Keyser	Compound larceny	"	"	"	
Edward Botsford	Larceny				

Names of persons prosecuted.	Offence charged.		
Judith Irish,	Lewd and lascivious cohabitation.	Oct., 1853.	$
Liberty Irish,	do	"	"
Wait. Frost,	Larceny.	"	"
William C. Hughes,	Nuisance.	"	"
William Wilson,	Escape.	"	"
Wallan Wilson,	Burglary.	Dec., 1853.	Convicted.
Buckly G. Bigbee, John M. Bigbee, Charles Bigbee, David Quirk, Edwin Chapman,	Riot.		Not disposed of.
Alexander Hurd, and others,	"		"
Ell Saubill, Bigbee Parker, Jackson Mann, John Clark,	Riot.		"
John Ostrander,	"		"
William D. Richards,	Malicious mischief.		"

Ottawa County—R. W. DUNCAN, ESQ., Prosecuting Attorney.

No Indictments found for the year ending November 30, 1853, in this county.

CLASS II.—CASES PROSECUTED OTHERWISE THAN BY INDICTMENT.

Names of persons prosecuted.	Offence charged.	Mode of prosecution.	In what court, whether before a justice or other magistrate.	When commenced.	When disposed of.	How disposed of, punishment, if any, or present condition of the case.
James Wiley,	Assault and battery.	Complaint.	Justice of the Peace.	Sept., 1853.	Sept., 1853.	Guilty—fined $5.
Milton E. Rawson,	"	do	do	Jan., 1853.	Jan., 1853.	Discharged.

Sanilac County—JOHN DIVINE, ESQ., Prosecuting Attorney.

CLASS I.—CASES PROSECUTED BY INDICTMENT.

Names of persons prosecuted.	Offence charged.	Month and year of indictment.	When disposed of.	How disposed of, punishment, if any, or present condition of the case.	Remarks.
Joseph Burley,	Rescue.	May, 1853.	May, 1853.	Convicted.	Imprisoned in county jail.
James Hopp,	Compound larceny.	"		Continued for trial.	
Isaac Coddington, John Brown, John Hunter and Wm. Warwick,	Larceny.	"		Not disposed of.	
Joseph Burke,	Crime against nature.	"		"	

4

CLASS II.—CASES PROSECUTED OTHERWISE THAN BY INDICTMENT.

Names of persons prosecuted	Offence charged	Mode of prosecution.	In what court, whether a justice or before a justice or other magistrate.	When commenced.	When disposed of.	How disposed of, punishment, if any, or present condition of the case.
Eli Summers,	Assault and battery.		Justice of the Peace.	Jan., 1853.	Jan., 1853.	Acquitted.
Lyman Covey,	"		do	March, 1853.	March, 1853.	"
Joseph Power,	Assault and indecent exposure.		do	May, 1853.	May, 1853.	County jail 30 days.
George Reynolds,	Assault and battery.		do	July, 1853.	July, 1853.	Fined $15.
C. Smith,	"		do	"	"	Recog. to circuit court.
George Stowell, William Clancy and George Burch,	"		do	Sept., 1853.	Sept., 1853.	Fined and imprisoned.
William Allen,	Larceny.		do	"	"	County jail 30 days.
Frank Palmater,	Assault and battery.		do	"	"	Fined $10.
Silas Bardwell,	Attempt to kill.		do	Oct., 1853.	Oct., 1853.	Acquitted.
George Jerome and Sarah Bradley,	Lewd and lascivious cohabitation.		do	Nov., 1853.	Nov., 1853.	"

Shiawassee County—LUKE H. PARSONS, ESQ., *Prosecuting Attorney.*

CLASS I.—CASES PROSECUTED BY INDICTMENT.

Names of persons prosecuted	Offence charged.	Month and year of indictment.	When disposed of.	How disposed of, punishment, if any, or present condition of the case.	Remarks.
William Mitchell,	Assault with intent to kill.	Oct., 1852.	Dec., 1852.	Acquitted.	
William Coof,	Trespass on State lands.	May, 1852.	May, 1853	Convicted.	Fined $5.
Jeremiah Coof,	"	"	"	Acquitted.	
Alexander Stevens,	Perjury.			Nolle Prosequi.	
Ephraim McLaughlin,	Keeping gambling house.	May, 1853.		Not disposed of.	
William Goss & Avery Thomas,	Misdemeanor.	"	Oct., 1853.	Nol. Pros.	Indictment quashed
William H. Doyn,	"	"		Not disposed of.	
Calvin Sweet,	Assault and battery.	Oct., 1853.		"	
John O'Neil and H. Wallace,	Malicious trespass.	"		"	
Jonathan Burk,	Assault with intent to commit rape.	"		"	Not arrested.
Perry Mattison,	Malicious trespass.	"		"	"

CLASS II.—CASES PROSECUTED OTHERWISE THAN BY INDICTMENT.

Names of persons prosecuted.	Offence charged.	Mode of prosecution.	In what court, whether before a justice or other magistrate.	When commenced.	When disposed of.	How disposed of, punishment, if any, or present condition of the case.
Allen Beard,	Assault and battery.	Complaint.	Justice of the Peace.	Feb., 1853.	Feb., 1853.	Discharged.
Augustus Peru,	Threats.	do	do	Jan., 1853.	Jan., 1853.	"
Sarah Culver,	"	do	do	March, 1853.	March, 1853.	Convicted, fined $25.
John M. Babbot,	Selling liquor.	do	do	April, 1853.	April, 1853.	" fine $5.
Palmer C. Card,	Assault and battery.	do	do	May, 1853.	May, 1853.	Acquitted.
Henry Kelly,	Larceny.	do	do	June, 1853.	July, 1853.	"
Simon Z. Kenyon,	Selling liquor to Indians	do	do	"	June, 1853.	"
—— Hyde,	"	do	do	Aug., 1853.	Aug., 1853.	Convicted, fine $50.
Frederick Keightly,	Larceny.	do	do	"	"	" fine $5.
Ezekiel VanWormer,	Assault and battery.	do	do	"	"	" fine $20.
Thomas Ellison,	Malicious trespass.	do	do	Sept., 1853.	Sept., 1853.	Convicted, jail 30 days.
—— Snow,	"	do	do	Nov., 1853.	Nov., 1853.	$10 fine.
Robert McLaughlin,	Assault and battery.	do	do	"	"	Escaped.
Henry Petts,	Adultery.	do	do	"	"	Not disposed of.
J. R. Sawyer,	Assault and battery.	do	do	"	"	"

St. Clair County—SMITH FALKENBURY, Esq., Prosecuting Attorney.

CLASS I.—CASES PROSECUTED BY INDICTMENT.

Names of persons prosecuted.	Offence charged.	Month and year of indictment.	When disposed of.	How disposed of, punishment, if any, or present condition of the case.	Remarks.
Reuben Wood & Stephen More,	Obstruction of highway.	May, 1852	Sept., 1852	Convicted.	
William Ward,	Perjury.	"	"	Indictment quashed.	
Ebenezer Westbrook,	Extortion.	"		Indictment lost.	
William S. Chrestwell,	Embezzlement.	"	Sept., 1852	Indictment quashed.	Fined $10.
Silas Parker and Sarah Parker,	Keeping house of ill fame	Nov., 1852		Not disposed of.	
Charles Ross Cameron,	Larceny.	March, 1853	May, 1853	Escaped.	
John Reynolds,	Seduction.	"		Nolle prosequi.	
Edward Suple,	Rape.	"		Not disposed of.	
James F. Harvey, et al.,	Wilful trespass.				
Corridon Harvey & John Greenman,		"	"	"	Sentenced to State prison 1 year.
Simon Locon,	Burglary.	"	March, 1853	Convicted.	" 2 years.
James Myers,	Larceny.	"	"	"	
John J. Falkenbury,	Perjury.	"	Sept., 1853	Indictment quashed.	

CLASS I.—[CONTINUED.]

Names of persons prosecuted.	Offence charged.	Month and year of indictment.	When disposed of.	How disposed of, punishment, if any, or present condition of the case.	Remarks.
Thomas Gorman,	Arson.	Sept., 1853.		Not disposed of.	
Franklin B. Frost and Amasa Scott,	Assault and battery.	Mar., 1853.	Sept., 1853.	Convicted.	Fined $20
William Strothers,	Adultery.	"	May, 1853.	Nolle prosequi.	

CLASS II.—CASES PROSECUTED OTHERWISE THAN BY INDICTMENT.

Names of persons prosecuted.	Offence charged.	Mode of prosecution.	In what court, whether or before a justice or other magistrate.	When commenced.	When disposed of.	How disposed of, punishment, if any, or present condition of the case.
William P. Fulton, Samuel Holliday and Mary Holliday,	Assault and battery.	Complaint.	Justice of the Peace.	May, 1853.	Jan., 1853.	Acquitted.
James L. Harvey, Harmon Kittredge, Lyman, Kittredge, Norman Ferguson and O. Hunily,	"	do	do			
Elijah Brown,	Wilful trespass.	do	do	Feb., 1853.	Feb., 1853.	Not disposed of.
Edward Long,	"	do	do	"	"	Jury disagreed.
John and Thomas Dooner,	Arson.	do	do	Jan., 1853.	Jan., 1853.	Held to bail.
Jewett Cameron,	Assault and battery.	do	do	March, 1853.	March, 1853.	Convicted, $50 fine.
Norman Wright and Freeman Loomis,	Larceny.	do	do	June, 1853.	June, 1853.	Imprisoned 10 dys in jail.
Daniel Wooden,	Assault and battery.	do	do	July, 1853.	July, 1853.	60 days jail, fine $25 each.
James C. Watson,	"	do	do	"	"	Acquitted.
Matzemskey Nusenburg,	Misdemeanor.	do	do	Sept., 1853.	Sept., 1853.	Convicted, fine $10.
Sehuyler J. Strickam, Jas Beach, John Kogan, Peter Nevin, John Hayes, James Huten, & Gabriel Garley,	"	do	do			$25 fine.
Smith Stekel,	Malicious mischief.	do	do	Oct., 1853.	Oct., 1853.	Held to bail.
Alfred Manchester,	Larceny.	do	do	Nov., 1853.	Nov., 1853.	Convicted, 20 days in jail.
Abraham Gough,	Threats.	do	do	"	"	Committed, fine $5.
J. Pound,	Assault and battery.	do	do	July, "	Aug., 1853.	Convicted, fine $5.
	"	do	do	Aug., 1853.		" fine $5.

St. Joseph County—CHARLES UPSON, Esq., Prosecuting Attorney.

CLASS I.—CASES PROSECUTED BY INDICTMENT.

Names of persons prosecuted.	Offence charged.	Month and year of indictment.	When disposed of.	How disposed of, punishment, if any, or present condition of the case.	Remarks.
Phillip Casper,	Larceny.	Dec., 1852.	Dec., 1852.	Acquitted.	No sentence passed.
Amos Casper,	"	"	"	Convicted.	
Thomas B. Barber,	Assault with intent to kill.	"		Not disposed of.	
Joseph Rob,	Fraud.	"		"	
Stacy D. Kneeler,	Seduction.	"		"	
John Plumer,	Passing counterfeit money.	"		"	
William Plumer,	"	"	Dec., 1852.	"	
Amos Casper,	Having counterfeit money in possession, with intent to pass the same.	"	"		Sentenced State prison 2 years.
William G. Strong.	Forgery.	April, 1851.	April, 1853.	Convicted.	Sentenced State prison 2 years.
Amos Parker,	Passing counterfeit money.	Dec., 1852.	"	Acquitted	
Horace Holden,	Perjury.	"	July, 1853.	"	
John L. Richardson,	Assault and battery.	"	April, "	Convicted.	Fined $100.
James D. Watson,	Perjury.	Sept., 1853.	Sept., 1853.	Acquitted.	
William Woodruff,	"	"	"	Nolle prosequi.	
Francis A. McCauley,	Aiding escape.	"		Convicted.	Sentenced to State Prison 2 years
Cornelius Bixby,	Receiving stolen property.	"		Not disposed of.	"
Lewis C. Osborne,	Seduction.	"		"	
Henry H. Whaley,	Malicious trespass.	"		"	
Washington E. Worthington,	"	"		"	
Thomas & David L. Smith,	Larceny.	"		"	
Francis A. McCauley,	Receiving stolen goods.	"		"	

CLASS II.—CASES PROSECUTED OTHERWISE THAN BY INDICTMENT.

Names of persons prosecuted.	Offence charged.	Mode of prosecution.	In what court, whether before a justice or other magistrate.	When commenced.	When disposed of.	How disposed of, punishment, if any, or present condition of the case.
E. H. Porter,	Passing counterfeit money.	Complaint.	Justice of the Peace.	Dec., 1852.	Jan., 1853.	Discharged.
Joseph Horton,	Assault and battery.	do	do	Jan., 1853.	"	Settled.
William and John Letts,	Threats.	do	do	"	"	Recog. to keep peace.
Evan Townsend,	Procuring abortion.	do	do	"		Not arrested.
Erastus A. Kingsbury,	Perjury.	do	do	Feb., 1853.	Feb., 1853.	Discharged.
William Sherwood,	Assault and battery.	do	do	"	"	Convicted, fined $40.
Jacob H. Hopkins,	"	do	do	"		Settled.
Nathan Slauson,	Passing counterfeit money.	do	do	March, 1853.	March, 1853.	Not arrested.

CLASS II.—[CONTINUED.]

Names of persons prosecuted.	Offence charged.	Mode of prosecution.	In what court, whether a justice or other magistrate.	When commenced.	When disposed of.	How disposed of, punishment, if any, or present condition of the case.
Andrew Wentherwax & Minor Isbell,	Larceny.	Complaint.	Justice of the Peace.	March, 1853.	March, 1853.	Convicted, fined $10.
Lewis E. Osborne,	Assault and battery.	do	do	April, 1853.	April, 1853.	"
William Mites & Levi Taylor,	"	do	do	Sept., 1853.	Sept., 1852.	" fined $15 each.
Cornelius Bixby,	Larceny.	do	do	June, 1853.	July, 1853.	Held to bail.
Henry H. Whaley,	Bastardy.	do	do	Aug., 1852.	Aug., 1853.	"
do	Seduction.	do	do	"	"	"
Washington E. Worthington,	Bastardy.	do	do	"	"	Discharged.
Luther Douglass,	Assault with intent to kill.	do	do	"	"	Held to bail
Selum M. Beall,	"	do	do	Sept., 1853.	Sept., 1853.	"
Francis A. McCauley,	Aiding escape.	do	do	"	"	Discharged.
Benjamin S. Boylston,	Murder.	do	do	"	"	Held to bail
Albert R. Southwaite,	Passing counterfeit money	do	do	Oct., 1853.	Oct., 1853.	"
John Clark,	"	do	do	"	"	"
John Williams,	"	do	do	Sept., 1853.	Sept., 1853.	"
William Wilson,	"	do	do	"	"	

Tuscola County—JOHN MOORE, ESQ., Prosecuting Attorney.

No Indictments found for the year ending November 30, 1853, in this county.

CLASS II.—CASES PROSECUTED OTHERWISE THAN BY INDICTMENT.

Names of persons prosecuted.	Offence charged.	Mode of prosecution.	In what court, whether a justice or before other magistrate.	When commenced.	When disposed of.	How disposed of, punishment, if any, or present condition of the case.
Thomas Lewis,	Assault and battery.	Complaint.	Justice of the Peace.	Jan., 1853.	Jan., 1853.	Acquitted.
Kibbee,	"	do	do	May, 1853.	May, 1853.	Convicted, fined $15.
Butler,	"	do	do	"	"	" fined $28.

Van Buren County—WILLIAM N. PARDEE, Esq., Prosecuting Attorney.

CLASS I.—CASES PROSECUTED BY INDICTMENT.

Names of persons prosecuted.	Offence charged.	Month and year of indictment.	When disposed of.	How disposed of, punishment, if any, or present condition of the case.	Remarks.
John White,	Burglary.	March, 1853.	March, 1853.	Convicted.	Sentenced 3 years in State Prison.
Sarahette Hathaway,	Larceny.	"	"	"	Judgment arrested.
Lorenzo Hathaway,	"	"	"	Acquitted.	
Manning S. Conkey,	Assault with intent to commit rape.	"	"	Hold to bail.	
Noah Dodge,	Assault and battery.	"	Sept., 1853.	Convicted.	Sentenced to State Prison 2 years.
Sarahette Hathaway,	Larceny.	Sept., 1853.	"	Acquitted.	
Lorenzo Hathaway,	"	"	"	Nol. Pros.	
John M. Reynolds,	Murder.	"	"	Convicted in first degree.	Sentenced to State Prison for life.

CLASS II.—CASES PROSECUTED OTHERWISE THAN BY INDICTMENT.

Names of persons prosecuted.	Offence charged.	Mode of prosecution.	In what court, whether a justice or before a justice or other magistrate.	When commenced.	When disposed of.	How disposed of, punishment, if any, or present condition of the case.	Remarks.
Lowel N. White,	Larceny.	Complaint.	Justice of the Peace.	June, 1853.	June, 1853.	Acquitted.	
Richard Manley,	Obtaining goods under false pretences.	do	do	July, 1853.	July, 1853.	Discharged.	

Wayne County—A. T. McREYNOLDS, Esq., Prosecuting Attorney.

CLASS I.—CASES PROSECUTED BY INDICTMENT.

Names of persons prosecuted.	Offence charged.	Month and year of indictment.	When disposed of.	How disposed of, punishment, if any, or present condition of the case.	Remarks.
James Stevens & Wm. Coffin,	Larceny.	March, 1853.	April, 1853.	Convicted.	Sentenced 3 years to State Prison.
Henry Croman,	"	"	"	Still pending.	
David Green,	"	"	"	Convicted.	" 5 " "
Thomas Ashton,	"	"	"	"	" 1 " "
Daniel C. Koef, Patrick Connoughton, James Daly and Edward O'Donell,	Larceny.	"	"	"	Each sent to county jail 3 months.
Robert Smith,	Assault and battery.	May, 1853.	May, 1853.	"	Fined $25.
Orange B. Potter,	Having counterfeit money with intent to pass the same.	"	"	Still pending.	
do	Passing counterfeit money.	"	......	......	

CLASS I.—[CONTINUED.]

Names of persons prosecuted.	Offence charged.	Month and year of indictment.	When disposed of.	How disposed of, punishment, if any, or present condition of the case.	Remarks.
James Barrow,	Altering public records.	May, 1852.		Still pending.	
Henry F. Church,	Perjury.	"		"	
John Pendugast and Timothy Mahony,	Assault and battery.	"		"	
Charles Hoag, Harriot Sly, Bett, Desalis, Clastique Cole, Mary Drake,	Keeping house of ill fame.	"		"	
Francis Pengussart and John Pendugast,	Assault and battery.	"		"	
Elizabeth Smith,	Keeping house of ill fame.	"		"	
Charles Lawrence and William Booker,	"	"		"	
Ann Boseley,	"	"		"	
Patrick Wheeler and Michael Lorin,	Assault and battery.	"		"	
William Martin,	False pretences.	"		"	
do	Larceny.	"		"	
John Dumas,	Manslaughter.	Sept., 1852.		"	
Mrs. Crowan and Timothy Lenahan,	Nuisance.	"		Nolle prosequi.	
Henry Ledgor,	Keeping gambling house.	May, 1853.		Still pending.	
Russell Gage,	Resisting an officer.	March, 1853.		"	
James Wilson,	Larceny.	"		"	
John Doe,	Keeping disorderly house.	"		"	
William Glaze,	Misdemeanor.	"	April, 1853.	Convicted.	Fined $75.
John Soward,	Larceny.	June, 1853.		Still pending.	
William Gaines and Benjamin Loughman,		April, 1853.		Nolle prosequi.	
John Thompson,	Embezzlement.			Still pending.	
Josiah Shroove,					
John Hackett, Thomas Hackett, Edward Reed and Sherman Sherwood,	Larceny.	March, 1852.	April, 1853.	Two Hacketts convicted, and new trial granted.	Reed and Sherwood escaped.
Honorabe Galaher,	"	"	"	Convicted.	Sentenced to State Prison 2 years.
John L. Hall,	Administering poison.	April, 1853.	April, 1853.	Acquitted.	
Joseph Wortman,	Assault with intent to commit rape.	"		Still pending.	
Matthew Moynahoe, J. Stewart, R. Salter and Wm. Donaldson,	Assault and battery.	"		"	

Names	Offense	When committed	When tried	Result	Sentence
Ensign Lrey	Forgery	"		"	
do	"	"		"	
Charles Tryon	Neglecting to pay over moneys collected	"		Nolle prosequi	
William Champ and John R. Wilcoxson	Assault with intent to rob	"	Nov., 1853.	Still pending	
Edward Blake and John Daly	Larceny	"	July, 1853.	Acquitted	
Thomas O'Donell & John Urch	"	"	April, 1853.	"	
Benjamin Kellogg	Nuisance	May, 1853.	"	Still pending	Fined $150.
Francis Wyls	Keeping house of ill fame	March, 1853.	"	Nolle prosequi	Sentenced to county jail 1 year.
Charles Bosely	Assault and battery	"	"	Convicted	State Prison 1 yr. & 6 mos.
Thomas Penney	Larceny	"			" 5 years.
Isaac Gaston	Rape	"	"	Still pending	Sentence suspended.
Thomas Hackett	Assault and battery	"	"	Convicted	"
David Penner	Breaking jail	"		"	"
Thomas Hackett	Breaking jail			"	
John Hackett, Thomas Hackett and John Schafer		May, 1853.	May, 1853.	"	Sentenced to State Prison.
Thomas Hackett, John Hackett and John Schafer		"	"	"	" 1 year.
John Canada		"	"	Still pending	" 6 months.
Patrick Spellman	Perjury	"	"	Convicted	" 10 years.
William H. Wheeler	Robbery	"	"		" 18 mos.
John Murry	Larceny	"	"	Acquitted	
David Feemer	Rape	"	"	Convicted	" 1 year.
Cornelius Barry	Grand larceny	"	"	Discharged	" county jail 4 months.
Alfred Loom	Rape	Nov., 1853.	April, 1853.	Convicted	
Charles Canapan	Larceny	"	"	Nolle prosequi	" State Prison 3 years.
John Bailey	Manslaughter	"	May, 1853.		
Egon Vanderbecker	Nuisance	"	April, 1853.	Still pending	
Phillip Peter	Larceny	March, 1853.	"	"	3 mos. county jail, and $100 fine.
George Heron	"	"		"	
Peter Barry	"	"		"	
Henry Cronin	"	"		"	
do	Assault and battery	"	May, 1853.	Convicted	Sentence suspended.
John Walker	Larceny	"		Still pending	
John Leonard	"	"		"	
Henry Ozoma					

5

CLASS I.—[CONTINUED.]

Names of persons prosecuted.	Offence charged.	Month and year of indictment.	When disposed of.	How disposed of, punishment, if any, or present condition of the case.	Remarks.
John Schaffer, Thomas Hackett and Charles Sheriff,	Larceny.	March, 1853.	May, 1853.	Convicted.	Sentence suspended.
William Gaines and Benjamin Loughman,	"	"	"	"	Sentenced to county jail 6 months.
Daniel Hays and John Haly,	"	"	"	"	Sentence suspended.
Daniel Hays and John Haly,	"	"	"	"	"
Dennis Dyning, Thomas Mack and Edward Blake,	"	"	"	Dyning & Blake convicted—Mack discharged.	Sentenced to county jail 10 days.
Edward Blake,	"	"	"	Convicted.	" State Prison 1 year.
Francis Dyning & Ed. Blake,	"	"	"	"	" " 3 years.
Edward Riley,	"	"	"	"	" " 1 year.
Henry Croom,	Larceny.	"	April, 1853.	Still pending.	" county jail 6 months.
do	"	"	"	Convicted.	Sentenced to State Prison on 3 indictments 12 years.
John Jones,	do	"	"	"	Sentenced to county jail 6 months.
James Stevens and Wm. Coffin,	"	"	"	"	" State Prison 1 year.
Charles Sheriff,	"	"	"	Indictment quashed.	" county jail 6 months.
Henry Ledyard,	Obstructing highway.	Sept., 1852.	May, 1853.	Convicted.	
Jacob Kesler,	Bastardy.	March, 1853.	"	"	
Simon Labadie,	Forcible entry.	June, 1853.	"		Fined $20.

RECAPITULATION.

CASES PROSECUTED BY INDICTMENT.

Total number of Indictments found, and embraced in this Report,..................339.

CRIMES.

Administering deadly poison,..	1
Adultery,...	3
Assault and Battery,..	31
Assault, with intent to kill,...	12
Assault, with intent to commit a rape,..	4
Assault, with intent to commit a robbery,...	1
Arson,..	4
Bastardy...	1
Bigamy,...	1
Breaking jail,..	4
Burglary,...	9
Crime against Nature,...	2
Embezzlement,...	5
Escape,...	4
Extortion,..	4
False Pretenses,..	12
Forcible Entry..	1
Forgery,..	5
Fraud,..	1
Having Counterfeit Money in possession, with intent to pass the same,...................	6
Incest,...	1
Illegal Voting,...	4
Keeping Gambling House,...	2
Keeping House of Ill Fame,..	6
Larceny,..	96
Lewd and Lascivious Co-habitation,..	4
Libel,..	5
Malicious Mischief,...	10
Malicious Trespass,...	6
Maintenance,..	1
Manslaughter,...	2
Misdemeanor,..	6
Murder,...	2
Neglecting to pay over moneys collected,..	1
Nuisance,...	11

Obstructing Highway,... 2
Passing Counterfeit Money,.. 10
Perjury,.. 24
Rape, ... 8
Resisting Officer,.. 2
Rescue,... 1
Riot.. 6
Receiving Stolen Goods,... 3
Robbery,.. 2
Seduction,.. 5
Selling Unwholesome Provisions,... 1
Trespass on State Lands,.. 4

    Total,.. 339

HOW DISPOSED OF.

Convicted and Imprisoned, or Fined,... 93
Still Pending,.. 198
Acquitted, ... 38
Under Recognizance,... 4
Nolle Prosequi,... 30
Indictments Quashed,.. 5
Escaped, ... 6
Not Arrested,... 2

    Total,.. 339

CASES PROSECUTED OTHERWISE THAN BY INDICTMENT.

Administering Deadly Poison,.. 1
Adultery, ... 2
Arson,.. 3
Assault and Battery,.. 184
Assault, with intent to kill,.. 10
Bastardy,... 3
Contempt of Court,.. 1
Disorderly Conduct,... 30
Disturbing Religious Meeting,... 1
Escape,... 1
False Pretenses,.. 7
Fraud,.. 5
Having Counterfeit Money in possession, with intent to pass the same,............. 1
Larceny,.. 64
Lewd and Lascivious Co-habitation,.. 2
Malicious Mischief,... 16
Murder, ... 1
Obstructing Highway,.. 2
Obstructing Railroad track,... 1
Passing Counterfeit money,.. 11
Perjury, ... 5

Procuring Abortion,... 1
Rape,... 1
Resisting Officer,.. 2
Seduction,... 3
Trespass on State Lands,.. 1
Threats of Personal Violence,.. 20
Vending Spirituous Liquors to Indians,.. 1
Vending Spirituous Liquors without License,... 9
Vending unwholesome Provisions,.. 1
                                                                              _____
    Total,.. 389
                                                                              ======

HOW DISPOSED OF.

Absconded,.. 7
Acquitted,... 43
Convicted and fined,.. 146
Convicted and sentenced to Imprisonment in County Jail,.............................. 50
Committed to County Jail for want of sureties, to keep the peace,..................... 4
Discharged,.. 34
Discontinued,.. 12
Not Arrested,.. 10
Recognised to apear at Circuit Court,.. 42
Recognized to keep the Peace,.. 27
Still Pending,... 14
                                                                              _____
    Total.. 389
                                                                              ======

TABLE, *showing the number of Convictions upon Indictments, and the period for which the convicted were sentenced to Imprisonment in the State Prison:*

COUNTIES.	6 Months	1 Year	18 Months	2 Years	3 Years	4 Years	5 Years	7 Years	10 Years	12 Years	15 Years	Life	Total
Allegan,	..	..	..	..	..	..	..	..	..	..	..	..	..
Barry,	..	..	..	..	1	..	..	..	..	..	..	..	1
Berrien,	..	..	..	..	..	..	1	..	1	..	..	..	2
Branch,	..	..	..	..	..	..	..	..	..	..	1	..	1
Calhoun,	..	..	..	..	..	..	1	..	..	..	..	..	1
Cass,	..	..	..	..	..	1	..	..	..	..	..	..	1
Clinton,	..	..	..	..	..	..	..	..	..	..	..	..	.
Eaton,	..	..	..	..	..	..	..	..	..	..	..	..	..
Genesee,	..	..	..	..	..	..	..	..	..	..	..	..	
Hillsdale,	..	..	..	..	..	3	.1	..	..	..	..	..	4
Ingham,	..	..	..	..	..	..	..	..	..	..	..	1	1
Ionia,	..	..	..	..	..	..	..	..	..	..	..	..	.
Jackson,	..	1	1	1	..	..	..	..	..	..	..	..	3
Lapeer,	..	..	..	..	..	..	..	..	..	..	..	..	.
Lenawee,	..	..	..	2	..	1	..	..	..	..	..	..	3
Livingston,	..	..	..	..	..	..	..	1	..	..	..	..	1
Macomb,	..	..	..	..	..	..	..	..	..	..	..	..	..
Monroe,	..	..	..	..	1	..	..	..	..	..	..	..	1
Oakland,	..	..	..	..	..	..	..	..	..	..	..	..	..
Ottawa,	..	..	..	..	..	..	..	..	..	..	..	..	
Sanilac,	..	..	..	..	..	..	..	..	..	..	..	..	
Shiawassee,	..	..	..	..	..	..	..	..	..	..	..	..	.
St. Clair,	..	1	..	1	..	..	..	..	..	..	..	..	2
St. Joseph,	..	..	..	3	..	..	..	..	..	..	..	..	3
Van Buren,	..	..	..	1	1	..	..	..	..	..	..	1	3
Wayne,	1	6	2	1	3	..	2	..	1	1	..	..	17
Total,													41